With every good wish

❧ ❧ ❧

*What Every Woman Should Know
About Investing Her Money*

❧ ❧ ❧

To HERB and LINDA

❧ ❧ ❧

What Every Woman Should Know About Investing Her Money

Herta Hess Levy

❧ ❧ ❧

DARTNELL
Chicago • London

⚜ ⚜ ⚜

Acknowledgments

I gratefully acknowledge the assistance of partners and associates of Paine, Webber, Jackson & Curtis: Charles O. Ames, Arthur W. Bullock, John G. Capps, Jr., Blev C. Dunklin, Harry A. Fischer, Jr., Robert B. Johnson, Marvin Krasnansky, Ilmar Mikiver, Daniel J. Reske, Harry Simanek, William R. Stanhope, Robert A. Sullivan, J. Peter Thompson, George Washburn, Gloria Wiener, Robert M. Wigod; also Alan J. Altheimer and Milton H. Gray of Altheimer, Gray, Naiburg, Strasburger & Lawton; Jack A. Cottle of Cottle & Cottle; Rosecrans Baldwin and Robert H. Monyek, partners in the firm of Arthur Young & Company; Marcelle Benson and Sally R. Campbell.

The opinions expressed in this book are those of the author.

HERTA HESS LEVY

❧ ❧ ❧

Contents

❦ ❦ ❦

Introduction

Twentieth Century Woman must be equipped for the age in which she lives. Her functions are as many and as complex as the demands on her time. Yet she should always be completely a woman . . . with the knowledge that intelligence animates rather than detracts from her charm and personality.

For the Twentieth Century Woman to be well-oriented financially is no longer a choice, but a necessity. It gives her additional poise and a true sense of security and equanimity to know that she can plan her financial present and future—by herself if need be—or in conjunction with partners, business or emotional. In short, she must understand and function efficiently in the economic environment in which she lives.

A tailor-made plan is a must. The renowned psychoanalyst, Franz Alexander, speaks of chronic fatigue as a modern curse. It is caused by four factors: fear, indecision, boredom, and a fainthearted, mean-spirited approach to life. Too many women show a venomous, antagonistic reaction to what is after all a delightful problem—what to do with money. A healthy and enlightened approach to such a problem is to find the counsel of professionals, to draw upon that counsel, and to live constructively and well, relatively untroubled.

You will find yourself among the type patterns discussed in this book if you can say . . .

I am a career girl.

I am a married woman—with or without income.

I am a widow.

I am prepared financially to follow an investment program tailored to my specific financial circumstances, age, and temperament.

Let's learn how!

CHAPTER 1

✤ ✤ ✤

Who Is
The Woman Investor?

Every woman is a potential investor. Women today are waking up to the economic world. Women collectively can take credit for well over 80 percent of consumer spending in the country. They own almost half the shares of common stock held by individuals and almost half of all the real estate. They are the beneficiaries of more than half of the life insurance policies written in addition to owning their own policies worth billions of dollars. Women also hold over one third of the nation's paying jobs and collect 20 percent of the wage and salary income.

There are several reasons for the vast amount of wealth in the hands of women. First, they tend to marry earlier and live longer than men—on the average, women outlive their husbands by about 10 years. Second, tax laws encourage trust funds and joint ownership of property, bringing more money to women. Third, more women are working —and at better jobs than in the past. They are more likely to save and invest at least a part of what they earn.

Now let's consider a few qualifying remarks on women and money. While women do in fact own almost half the securities in the country and are the main beneficiaries of life insurance, they do *not*, for the most part, control their own wealth—either because they choose to let someone else manage their money or because they have inherited funds, but do not control their use. Perhaps half of the wealth owned by women is managed by someone else. Women possess wealth, receive income from it, enjoy its benefits—but have little control over or even understanding of the management of money.

Women are an economic force by the mere possession of money. Yet, they have not learned to apply imagination and creativity in the use of money. Funds invested for and by women are for the most part invested conservatively.

The woman of today has more and better education than her counterpart of 20 years ago. Consequently, she is prepared to take an active part in every phase of modern living. The numerous choices and possibilities open to her were unavailable to women in the past. Today's woman can choose from any number of careers. Even marriage is more a matter of choice than of economic necessity today. A woman can combine marriage, motherhood, and a career. She can decide when and if she wants children. Now women can find satisfaction not only in the home and in family life but also on the job, in the community, socially, and certainly in the financial world.

Members of the female sex normally respond to problems of money management in different ways. There is the rare woman who is both thoroughly feminine and thoroughly knowledgeable in financial matters—the one attribute does not interfere with the other. This woman has complete regard and respect for her financial counselors, yet makes her own decisions on the use of her money—based, of course, on sound advice and information. She moves knowingly through the investment world, yet manages to be completely feminine and charming.

Another type of woman is totally out of touch with the money world. Her lack of understanding of matters financial is almost alarming. She may be well educated—up on the theater, literature, art—have the last word on raising children or decorating her home—but this woman's knowledge of economics centers around spending. When faced with investment decisions, this woman would buy stock in Sara Lee because its cake tastes good—sell American Airlines because her last flight was delayed—hang on to a stock for dear life because it was given to her as a wedding present. Such women fail to grasp the fundamentals of investing.

Any reasonably intelligent woman can learn her way around the money world and at the same time preserve her feminine nature. In so doing, she can achieve not only greater financial security but greater emotional security. She will become a more interesting companion for the intelligent men and women around her.

The Shareowner: A Profile

Who owns shares in publicly held companies? Let's take a brief look at American investors as seen in the *Census of Shareowners* compiled by the New York Stock Exchange. In 1965 shareholders numbered over 20 million—one in every six adults. Thirteen million households owned stock—with an average of 1.5 shareowners per house. Holdings of all individual owners were valued at approximately $400 billion. Of the 20 million shareowners, 18.5 million were adults—9 million men and 9.4 million women. Women outnumbered men 51 percent to 49 percent. The average investor, according to the census, owned from three to four different issues.

Of the total shareowners, 1.3 million were minors. Individuals 65 years and older made up almost 17 percent of the total and the age group from 35 to 54 accounted for 8.9 million or 45 percent.

The median income of America's shareowners was just under $10,000. The largest single income group of shareholders earned between $10,000 and $15,000 annually. Stockownership was only one form of investment for most shareholders—88 percent had savings accounts; 88 percent had life insurance; 79 percent were homeowners; 56 percent participated in pension plans; 53 percent held U.S. savings bonds; 12 percent held other bonds.

Of the 20 million shareowners in the U.S. almost two-thirds owned issues listed on the New York Stock Exchange. Sixteen percent owned only investment company shares; 15.6 percent held issues sold in the over-the-counter market; 6.4 percent owned stock listed on other exchanges.

In considering investors by occupation, housewives were the largest single group. They numbered well over six million, more than 34 percent of the total. Of the employed women shareholders one in every two worked in sales or clerical jobs—one in four held professional or technical positions.

The woman investor is the young woman on her first job with small amounts to invest. She is the established career woman with an annual bonus or profit-sharing funds to invest. She is a married woman with income of her own to invest. She is in business for herself with profits to invest. She is a widow with an inheritance or other funds for investing. Or, she is a housewife sharing with her husband the pleasures of planning the family's financial future.

Yes, every woman is a potential investor. Some have no definite investment program—no plans for present or future financial security—no apparent aptitude for functioning effectively in the money world. Some women have an investment program of sorts—a vague idea of what they want to do with their "investable" money. Still others turn over their financial decisions to advisors and take little active interest in the results. A few refuse advice and run the show alone. The confident and most successful woman investor gets all the advice she can find and then makes her own informed decisions—perhaps with the help of one or more financial experts.

Starting Young

Let's begin with the young girl on her first job. Her future is uncertain. Maybe she will marry—maybe not. What can she gain from buying securities? How can she plan for an uncertain future? Why should she not enjoy her money and let the man she marries take care of the financial problems? The answers are obvious. Maybe she won't marry. If she does, a few dollars of her own would be as welcome—perhaps more welcome—when she is married than now. Certainly if she invests some money now—if she learns the ins and outs of the investment world—she will be a more competent partner when she does marry. She will be prepared to plan a financial future with her husband—to share this substantial and rewarding aspect of married life. If she does not marry, she will be able to provide for her own financial security—for the type of life she wants to live once her earning power subsides. She will be more confident as a woman and as a person in the knowledge that she is truly independent.

The established career woman without marriage plans has little choice in the matter of investing or not investing. If she wants a future with the necessities and luxuries to which her income has accustomed her, she simply must plan for the days when her earning power falls off. In addition to providing financial security, the career woman very often finds the investment world exciting and sustaining. The career woman who is in business understands many of the fundamentals of the stock and bond world before she enters it through personal experience. For her it may be a relatively short step from the sidelines to managing her personal income, buying securities, controlling her investment portfolio.

The married woman with income of her own—from either a job or inheritance—is in a delightful position in that most of her income will usually be discretionary—that is—available to spend on things other than necessities. She can very often take greater risks with her investment dollars—provided of course that she builds a foundation of sound securities. Ideally, she and her husband will work out an investment plan together. Perhaps because part of the money invested is her own, the married woman with independent income frequently takes an active interest in putting together an investment portfolio with her husband.

The widow with inherited funds to invest may be in one of several positions, depending on how much she shared in making family financial decisions, how much she knows about her husband's

16

financial planning, how much she has inherited, and what control she has over the inheritance. The widow whose previous knowledge and experience in managing income and investments are limited or virtually nonexistent is in an unfortunate situation. She has to learn quickly the fundamentals that she would be better off already knowing, or—the alternative—turn over her financial matters to someone else, thus being robbed of the satisfaction that comes from managing her own investment portfolio.

The widow who has some knowledge of her husband's investment program and his financial plans for her and the family is in a better situation. She has less to learn and can move more easily to the helm. If she prefers not to take over personally, at least she can observe intelligently and understand what her financial advisors are doing. She will feel more in control of her financial life and consequently more secure.

The widow who shared financial planning with her husband, who took part in managing the family income, who fully understands what is involved in putting together a sound, effective investment portfolio—will be able to move smoothly into the role of financial manager. And in carrying out the financial plans she and her husband started together, she may be able to make the emotional adjustment to widowhood more readily. She at least will not have the helpless feeling of being totally dependent on advisors. She will know just where she stands financially.

While every woman is a potential investor, not every woman does in fact enter the investment world. Some invest indirectly, so to speak—through insurance, pension funds, mutual funds, or through the decisions of husbands, advisors, or counselors.

What are the requirements for becoming a true, confident, successful—yet feminine—woman investor? First, motivation—you must have the desire to become an investor and to see the wonderful things your money can do. Next, you must understand a few basic economic facts—how the economy works, how the securities market works, what investment terms mean, how to interpret economic news, where to go for information. Then you will want to set up your investment *goals*—what you hope to get from your investment dollars—and learn which types of securities will be most effective in reaching your goals. You will want to learn some of the more advanced financial things to know that help you make investment choices. Of course—even when you become an expert—you will need to know how to work with the professionals who serve you:

the broker, investment counselor, banker, accountant, attorney.

The best investment program for *you* depends on your financial situation—your goals, the amount you have to invest—now and in the future. What is your earning power? How long can you expect to earn money? What are your financial commitments to family, mortgage, other debts? How much of your income is required for living costs? How much have you set aside for emergencies and unexpected expenses? Are you adequately insured against major economic risks? How much do you have left to invest or spend in other ways? How much are you willing to invest or save in order to live as you would like to live in the future? What are the best investment possibilities for the funds you have to invest and the goals you have in mind?

Some of these questions you can answer yourself, but few of us have all the answers. The best way to start an effective long-range investment plan is to seek out basic information—much of it you will find in this book. Next get the advice of experts on where, when, and how to invest your money. Finally, and perhaps most importantly, be informed and discriminating about the advice you follow and the securities you buy.

CHAPTER 2

✤ ✤ ✤

The Securities
Markets

The collective investments of millions of Americans finance the business world. Every individual has an opportunity to own an interest in American enterprise—and to share in the economic growth of the nation. Business relies on the public for funds to buy plant, equipment, and materials—for consumers to buy what is produced. The public depends on business for goods and services and for jobs. Different industries depend on each other. Government and business are interdependent. Consider the relationships between farmers, labor, management, government, and consumers. None could exist and function financially or otherwise without the other. The financial relationships between the business world and the investor are carried out primarily through the securities market. It is here that the public invests the money that finances business expansion and growth. It is here that the public seeks to share in the growth of the economy and of the companies in which it invests.

The Securities Market

Essentially the securities market is a place to buy and sell securities. Generally speaking, you can trade two types of securities—bonds and stocks. Bondholders are actually creditors of the corporation issuing the bonds. As such, they are entitled to a fixed rate of return on their investment which must be paid whether business is good or bad—and paid *before* stockholders receive any dividend. Stockholders on the other hand are part owners of the business and share in the profits. The stockholder's return on his investment depends on the company's earnings—his returns are high when business is good but low or nonexistent when business is poor.

Normally bonds are considered a more conservative investment than stocks. However, the financial condition of the business issuing the securities is the most important factor to consider for both safety and earning potential of stocks or bonds. The stocks of some companies are a safer investment than the bonds of others. It pays to learn all you can about a company before buying any of its securities. In

Chapter 6 you will find a fuller explanation of the types of stocks and bonds you can buy and how to select those best suited to your investment goals.

Stock Exchanges

Any securities you buy will be traded either through a stock exchange or over the counter. A stock exchange is a center for trading the securities listed on that exchange. It operates like a two-way auction—buyers and sellers compete. The buyer who makes the highest bid buys from the seller with the lowest offer when the two agree on a price. Some 3,000 securities are traded in this way on stock exchanges in the United States. There are 14 exchanges registered with the Securities and Exchange Commission:

American Stock Exchange

Boston Stock Exchange

Chicago Board of Trade

Cincinnati Stock Exchange

Detroit Stock Exchange

Midwest Stock Exchange

National Stock Exchange

New York Stock Exchange

Pacific Coast Stock Exchange

Philadelphia-Baltimore-Washington Stock Exchange

Pittsburgh Stock Exchange

Salt Lake Stock Exchange

San Francisco Mining Exchange

Spokane Stock Exchange

In addition to these are the Colorado Springs Stock Exchange, the Honolulu Stock Exchange and the Richmond Stock Exchange. These are not registered with the SEC, but must meet certain requirements to operate.

Most securities traded on an exchange are listed —that is issued by corporations meeting the exchange's requirements for listing. The corporation applies for listing and agrees to comply with the exchange's regulations and to furnish periodic financial reports and other requested information. Each exchange sets up its own requirements for listing securities. To list its stocks or bonds, a corporation must also register securities with the Securities and Exchange Commission. Some exchanges permit trading in a few issues not formally listed.

The New York Stock Exchange, sometimes called the "Big Board," is the largest organized securities market in the nation. The exchange is located on Broad and Wall Streets in New York City. This financial center of the world was once the nation's political capital.

On Wall Street, Washington took the first Presidential oath of office, the first Continental Congress gathered, the Bill of Rights was adopted. In 1789-90, Congress authorized an $80 million stock issue to help pay for the Revolutionary War. This stock and the shares of beginning banks and insurance companies were bought and sold in coffee houses, auction rooms, and offices. The market was unorganized and investors were reluctant to buy securities that they might have difficulty selling at a later date. The New York Exchange was established to solve the problem.

A group of 24 merchants and auctioneers decided to sell and buy securities at certain hours each day under a now famous buttonwood tree on Wall Street. These 24 brokers, the original members of the exchange, handled buy and sell orders for the public. In 1793 the exchange moved indoors to the newly completed Tontine Coffee House, also on Wall Street. Trading grew and market activities increased steadily after the War of 1812. The Industrial Revolution brought new enterprises and desirable investment opportunities. In 1817 the members of the exchange met the need for a more formal organization by adopting the first constitution of the New York Stock and Exchange Board. This agreement called for the president to fix commissions on the sale of securities, set fines for violation of procedures, and call out the names of stocks each morning for brokers to make their bids and offers. The exchange moved from place to place until reaching its present location in 1863.

Today the New York Stock Exchange exists as an

unincorporated association. It is governed by a 33-man board of governors—29 members and allied members—together with a president and three governors elected by the board to represent the public point of view. The board of governors guides the policies and programs of the exchange.

Exchange membership is set at 1,366. Of the 649 NYSE member organizations, 484 are partnerships and 165 are corporations. Membership requirements are strict. To become a member candidates must:

- Meet standards of integrity set up by the exchange.
- Buy a "seat" at the price agreed upon between buyer and seller.
- Meet approval of the board of governors.
- Pass an examination before using membership privileges.

Members and member firms must also meet certain minimum capital requirements. Each year they are required to answer three financial questionnaires issued by the exchange. One is based on a surprise audit of the member firm's books. Spot checking is done to see that firms observe the regulations of federal and state governments and the exchange. While the exchange does not guarantee the solvency of members, financial statements are available. Also, members and member firms must carry fidelity bonds. Only members may execute orders on the NYSE.

Listings on the Big Board

Securities must be listed to be traded on the NYSE. The exchange lists some 2,900 issues—stocks and bonds of about 1,200 business enterprises including most leading corporations in the country —General Motors, Ford, Sears-Roebuck, Standard Oil, U.S. Steel. Together, the companies listed on the Big Board account for about one half of U.S. production each year, provide jobs for about 15 million people, pay stockholders over half of all dividends distributed in the country, and pay approximately $15 billion in taxes each year.

To be listed on the New York Exchange companies must normally show earning power of over $2 million annually before taxes and over $1.2 million after taxes and charges. They must have a minimum of one million shares outstanding with not less than 2,000 stockholders owning 700,000 or more of the shares—1,700 of the 2,000 must be round-lot (100 shares, or multiples thereof) stockholders. The aggregate market value of publicly held common shares should be at least $12 million.

In addition to these requirements, the exchange considers the national interest in a company, the market for its product, its position in its industry, and its relative stability. Before being listed companies must agree to publish earnings statements quarterly as well as an annual report. Practically all listed companies publish earnings statements at least four times each year. Once companies are listed they must still apply to the exchange before issuing new shares. After the initial listing, companies that do not maintain standards set by the exchange can be delisted.

Only companies that issue voting stock can be listed on the Big Board. The voting rights of shareholders must be in proportion to their ownership in the company. To make voting rights meaningful, the exchange insists that companies solicit proxies. This makes it possible for shareholders to register votes without personally attending all of the meetings called to make important company decisions.

The American Stock Exchange ranks second among the exchanges in the United States. It is similar to the NYSE in operation, but its listing requirements are not as stringent. The American Stock Exchange has been a particularly effective marketplace for newer stock issues, although its listings include large well-established corporations as well as smaller new businesses.

Buying and selling securities on any stock exchange is a speedy, efficient process. You can buy and sell shares in corporations almost as easily and quickly as you can deposit money in the bank—whether you live in a city, in a suburb, or on a farm.

Here's how it works. Suppose you live in St. Louis and want to buy 100 shares of AZ common stock, listed on the New York Stock Exchange. At about the same time, Mr. Thompson in Detroit, a complete stranger to you, decides to sell 100 shares of AZ.

You ask your broker for the quote on AZ, and, with the aid of an electronic device on his desk, he is able within seconds to tell you that the stock is 21¼ to 21½, last 21¼. That means that 21¼ is the highest anyone is willing to pay for AZ at the moment; 21½ is the lowest anyone is willing to sell it for; and the last sale was 21¼.

With this information in hand, you instruct your broker to buy 100 shares of AZ "at the market"—the best possible price at the time. In the meantime, Mr. Thompson has given his broker instructions to sell 100 shares of AZ at the market.

The two orders are wired to New York where floor brokers for the two firms take them to the post at the exchange where AZ is traded. There they learn that AZ is quoted $21\frac{1}{4}$ to $21\frac{1}{2}$. At this point, the broker representing you could accept the offer of $21\frac{1}{2}$ or the broker representing Mr. Thompson could accept the bid of $21\frac{1}{4}$. However, each broker wants to get the best possible price for his customer, so, instead, your broker bids $21\frac{3}{8}$, an eighth of a point below the current offering price. Seeing an opportunity to sell Mr. Thompson's 100 shares an eighth of a point higher than the current bid, his broker shouts "Sold," and the transaction is made.

This process is known as the auction market. The exchange has nothing to do with fixing the price of securities; it merely provides the place for you and Mr. Thompson to get together via your stockbrokers. The price is established by the law of supply and demand. Millions of buy and sell agreements are made in this way each year.

The Over-the-Counter Market

The over-the-counter market provides a place to negotiate the sale of unlisted securities—that is stocks and bonds not listed on any exchange. While listed securities may also be traded on the over-the-

counter market, this market deals primarily in unlisted securities, the distribution of new issues, and
the marketing of exceptionally large holdings of a
single security. The securities of approximately
40,000 companies are quoted on the over-the-counter
market. These securities include the stocks of most
bank and trust companies, insurance companies, and
real estate firms. Government obligations, or *governments* as they are called, and *municipals*, the obligations of state, county, and local governments, are
also traded in the over-the-counter market.

The over-the-counter market is made up of some
4,300 securities houses and 4,700 branch offices.
Trading is done over a vast network of telephones.
The securities houses that do business in the over-
the-counter market include:

- *Investment banking houses* which specialize in
  underwriting and distributing new issues.

- *Over-the-counter houses* which trade corporate
  and foreign securities in the over-the-counter
  market—they are not members of any ex·
  change.

- *Exchange member firms* which are members of
  exchanges but also trade in the over-the-counter market.

- *Government bond houses* which specialize in trading U.S. government obligations.

The *dealer* is the backbone of the over-the-counter market. He buys and sells for his own account and risk. It is the dealer who makes the market by quoting the prices at which he is willing to buy or sell the securities he trades. The dealer may also act as a broker—that is he may buy and sell for the account and risk of a customer and charge a commission for his services.

To *make a market* in a specific security, a dealer must know where he can obtain and dispose of it quickly and he must be prepared to build up an inventory of that security for trading. A dealer is said to have a position in a security when he has an adequate inventory for trading. He maintains a market in that security by buying and selling against his position. The dealer makes his profit from the *spread* or the difference between bids and offers.

Buying and selling in the over-the-counter market differs from transactions on the exchange. The OTC is essentially a negotiated market. Suppose you want to buy 50 shares of BC Corporation which sells on the OTC market. You call your broker and ask for *the market* in that security. This means you want a price quotation. Your broker will check the

AUTHOR HERTA LEVY spends most of her working day at this desk in the Chicago board room of Paine, Webber, Jackson & Curtis. While on the telephone with customers, she is in constant touch with prices from principal securities and bond markets. A desk-top computer gives instant data on earnings, yield, etc. Below is the New York Stock Exchange, Broad and Wall Streets, with statue of George Washington in foreground.

OVERLOOKING the packed trading floor of the New York Stock Exchange, two boys watch the action from the visitor's gallery. Admission for visitors is free, and an expert guide is supplied. Below, one of 18 U-shaped trading posts at which member brokers buy and sell stocks for millions of investors.

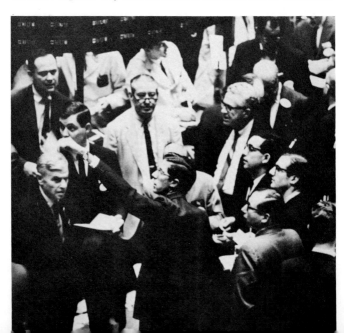

THE STOCK TICKER has undergone many changes since its invention in 1867. Thomas Edison's glass-domed ticker was a familiar sight for years. Today's improved "900" ticker (above, right), prints market transactions as fast as 900 characters per minute. Engineers (below, left), inspect the open back of a special voice assembler unit in the NYSE computer center. This converts stock quotations into spoken messages. Below, right, are computers in the Midwest Stock Exchange, Chicago.

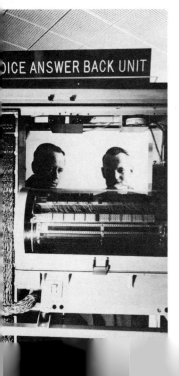

WALL STREET was named for an old Dutch wall (top right), with sharpened palisades which protected the 17th century colony from Indians. In 1792 a group of merchants and auctioneers met under a buttonwood tree on Wall Street to organize what was to become the New York Stock Exchange. Trading sessions were held outdoors for a year before moving into the Tontine Coffee House, depicted below.

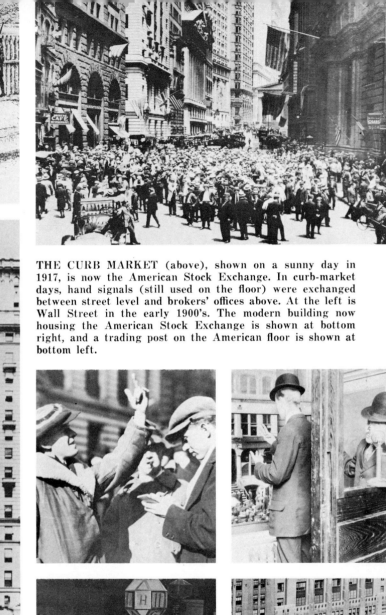

THE CURB MARKET (above), shown on a sunny day in 1917, is now the American Stock Exchange. In curb-market days, hand signals (still used on the floor) were exchanged between street level and brokers' offices above. At the left is Wall Street in the early 1900's. The modern building now housing the American Stock Exchange is shown at bottom right, and a trading post on the American floor is shown at bottom left.

THE PACIFIC COAST Stock Exchange is a consolidation of the Los Angeles and San Francisco stock exchanges. The exchange brings modern investor services to the two great metropolitan areas of California. The chaste architecture of the Pacific Coast Stock Exchange building at 301 Pine Street, San Francisco, is shown above. At the right is the more ornately columned exchange building at 618 South Spring Street in Los Angeles. Below is the trading floor of the Pacific Coast Stock Exchange in San Francisco. Note the large gallery for visitors (upper right of photo). College and high-school students in economics courses are frequent guests of the Pacific Coast exchange.

THE IMPOSING columned entrance to the Midwest Stock Exchange building is pictured above. Midwest is located at 120 South LaSalle Street, in the heart of Chicago's financial district. Below, center, is shown a part of Midwest's modern electronic data-processing system, which can edit, calculate, and assemble information for 5,000 transactions in 1½ hours. At the bottom, a direct phone line from Chicago to Cleveland is being used by Midwest floor brokers.

IT'S ALL PAPER! That shown in the photo above is in the form of common-stock certificates, representing ownership in American corporations. Below: Any homemaker will appreciate this photo of one way to "clean up on Wall Street." More than a ton of litter is left on the floor after every trading day on the New York Stock Exchange.

market for that stock by getting in touch with the houses that make a market for BC Corporation. He asks for bids and offers. In this way he finds out which house has the highest bid price and the lowest offering price, so that he can get the highest price if you are a seller and the lowest price if you are a buyer.

Suppose the highest bid is 35½ and the lowest offer is 36. If you feel that 36 is a reasonable offer, you may give your broker an order to buy 50 shares at 36. Then your broker will call the dealer with the lowest offering price once more to check the market. If the offer of 36 is still open, he will ask for *the size of the market*—this means how much stock is available at the quoted price. If he can buy the stock you want at 36, he may bid 35½ hoping to get your shares for less. If the dealer really wants to sell, he may come through with an offer of 35¾ and you have a savings of $12.50—25c per share less than your original bid. All of this may take no more than a few minutes. The procedure for selling is much the same.

Regulation of the Securities Market

The over-the-counter market is regulated by state laws as well as the Securities and Exchange Commission. In addition to such regulation, the National Association of Securities D e a l e r s, Inc. (NASD) was authorized by an act of Congress to make and enforce rules for member brokers and dealers. The association is devoted to maintaining the highest standards of conduct and ethical practices in the securities business for the protection of investors.

The Securities and Exchange Commission (SEC), established under the Securities Exchange Act of 1934, regulates the buying and selling of securities and protects the investing public from fraudulent, unethical procedures in the securities market. The SEC does not advise the investor on the worth of a particular security, but it does require that certain facts be made known so that investors can be informed before buying securities. The SEC administers the Securities Act of 1933 which requires that corporations selling new issues of stock to the public provide investors with a complete statement of pertinent information related to company operations. The SEC also administers the Securities Exchange Act of 1934, the Public Utility Holding Company Act of 1935, the Trust Indenture Act of 1939, the Investment Company Act of 1940, and the Investment Advisers Act of 1940.

CHAPTER 3

✤ ✤ ✤

Basic Economic Facts

Pick up almost any newspaper or magazine and you'll find something about the economy. "Consumer prices continue to rise." "Auto sales drop 4.5%." "Housewives rebel—picket supermarkets." "Consumer plans for major purchases decline." "Federal Reserve restricts money supply." "Business growth slows, inflation peril eases." The economy is reported strong, healthy, advancing—or you hear talk of recession or inflation. The market is bearish or it's bullish. What does it all mean?

Surveys show that few people really understand the meaning of these economic happenings. The average person would have some trouble defining common economic terms and phrases such as private enterprise, common stock, supply and demand, capitalism, inflation. These same studies also indicate that people would like to learn more about the economy and the way it operates.

Let's face it—we live in an economic world. Economic matters have a bearing on practically every aspect of national life. Economic trends also affect your personal life. They determine wages and prices, the cost of living, and the standard of living for American families. Today no one can afford to ignore the world of business and finance. It affects each person's pocketbook, security, and way of life. The better you understand how the economy functions, the more effectively you can handle your own financial affairs. You can take an active rather than passive interest in the economic things happening around you. Let's start by running through a few basic facts about the economy.

First, ours is a private-enterprise economy—owned and controlled largely by individuals rather than by government. Billions of dollars invested by American people make it possible for the U.S. to produce more goods and services than any other country in the world. Our free-enterprise system involves every individual in his role as producer and user of goods and services. Each time you use your telephone, buy groceries, earn money, borrow money, or invest your savings, you are playing a part in the overall operation of the national economy. Every man and woman—as a worker earning money and a consumer spending it—helps determine the success or failure of business. The total impact of all these factors is reflected in what economists refer to as economic indicators.

Economic Indicators

Economic indicators show how the economy has performed in the past and what it is likely to do in the future—judging by past performance. Once you understand and are able to interpret economic indicators, they can help you make investment decisions.

Indicators give a statistical picture of the economy—particularly production, employment, earnings, and spending. Statistical data is compiled by research departments of financial institutions, government agencies, and trade and business associations. The data is published in the financial pages of newspapers and business magazines, in market letters of brokerage firms, and in government bulletins.

Economic indicators are helpful to you in the sense that they provide a clue to the prospects for the economy and for specific industries. By relating this information to the companies in which you are interested as investments, you can evaluate their potential.

Economic information may be presented in a variety of forms. Statistical data frequently appears in tabular form. To be meaningful, the information should include the latest figures together with comparative figures for a previous period and the previous year or years. Economic indicators that can be of the greatest value to you in making investment decisions include those related to production, distribution, employment, and income.

Production indicators tell you something of the overall movement of the economy. Of these indicators, *Gross National Product (GNP)* is the best overall measure of economic growth. It tells the total national output of goods and services at market prices. The Department of Commerce reports the GNP quarterly at annual rates. Since 1950, our GNP has increased from $285 billion to $740 billion in 1966—an increase of approximately 160 percent. Gross National Product shows two things (1) the record of current spending and (2) the total of consumer, business, and government spending. This information can help investors estimate future business trends.

The *Industrial Production Index* reported by the Federal Reserve Board each month is another measure of the economy. It shows production in those industries that produce about one third of the nation's income. It also shows the combined and individual output of mining and utility industries and of major manufacturing industries, including metals, lumber, instruments, furniture, textiles, apparel, paper, chemicals, food and beverages, tobacco, rubber and plastics, and petroleum. The FRB Index does not cover important economic activities in construction, transportation, trade, and agriculture.

Other significant economic indicators include those related to specific key industries—steel, automotive, and petroleum. These indicators show output in the major industries of the nation, and are important because they have an effect on the outlook for all other industries and the overall economy.

In addition to actual production statistics, other figures show general trends in productive activity. The index, *Average Hours Worked Per Week in Manufacturing,* shows the manpower employed by different industries. The *Wholesale Price Index* gives price trends of materials used in most industries. The *Freight Car Loadings* Index reflects business trends related to the volume of raw materials and finished products shipped by rail.

Employment figures are another important measure of the economy. When employment is up, consumer spending tends to rise. People spend more for autos, appliances, amusements, food, clothes, services, and "nonnecessities." This boosts corporate sales and earnings. On the other hand, when employment drops, spending also falls off—particularly for durable goods and major purchases.

Disposable Personal Income figures measure consumers' ability to buy goods and services. Income figures include wages, salaries, dividends, interest, Social Security, and unemployment compensation—after taxes. Disposable personal income rose from $207 billion in 1950 to $505 billion in 1966—an increase of 144 percent. During the same period income per capita jumped from $1,364 to $2,567—an 87 percent increase.

Personal consumption figures may also have some meaning for the investor in that they indicate how consumers are spending their income, and consequently which industries are likely to profit most from the sale of consumer goods.

Economic indicators move up and down as a result of forces operating within the economy. Temporary ups and downs can be caused by strikes, weather conditions, and political forces. Major strikes can depress the earnings of specific companies and sometimes entire industries. When prolonged, a strike in a key industry such as airlines or steel will seriously affect general business conditions. For instance, the airline strike in the summer of 1966 brought severe consequences for many industries.

Weather extremes which bring crop failures not only lower farm income, but if serious, may also cause a drop in farm machinery sales. Eventually, food prices go up and sales in food industries suffer. Economic policies of government affect every industry. Business confidence and plans for expansion depend largely on the administration's policies in regard to taxes, government spending, labor relations, tariffs, and subsidies. Pending legislation for the regulation of business activity also affects many industries. For example, the Truth-In-Packaging Bill had a tremendous impact on the food industry—in possibly higher costs of packaging, marketing methods, advertising, etc. Auto-safety requirements seriously affected the automobile industry.

Some forces within the economy have a long-lasting or even permanent influence on business trends. Today one of the most important factors in our economic outlook is the *population growth*. By 1975, the U.S. population is expected to reach over 215 million; by the year 2000, it will be well over 300 million. This will bring higher employment, larger incomes, and an increase in the sale of consumer goods and services. It will also increase our GNP. If growth is accompanied by higher educational standards, the population will be demanding better jobs, earning more money, and buying better goods and services. To the investor, this means overall economic growth and greater earnings for the companies producing and selling consumer products.

Inflationary trends also have a long-lasting effect on the economy. Inflation results when demand and purchasing power increase faster than the output of goods and services. In this situation, prices go up because demand increases at a greater rate than the supply of things to buy. The final result is that increased prices cut down the buying power of the dollar. During periods of inflation GNP, employment, and personal income figures tend to go up as production tries to keep pace with demand.

Foreign trade has a long-lasting effect on business indicators. In export markets, low-priced foreign products competing with higher-priced American goods tend to reduce sales and earnings of industries that export products for sale in foreign markets. In the same way low-priced imports, such as we have seen with Japanese radios and television sets, can cut into domestic sales of some companies.

Defense spending affects production and employment figures. In 1966 total expenditures for national defense reached approximately $70 billion—over half of the federal budget. Increases in defense spending mean better sales and earnings in those industries that produce, manufacture, or sell electronic equipment, missiles, aircraft, ships, raw materials, and military supplies.

Research on new products brings production and earning figures up in certain industries—chemicals, electronic equipment, pharmaceuticals, transportation. Research expenditures by government, industry and universities increased 240 percent in the 10-year period from 1954 to 1964. Think of the products developed through research that we take for granted, many rare or nonexistent 20 years ago—electric blankets, TV, jet aircraft, electric appliances from can openers to microwave ovens, synthetic and stretch fabrics.

You can use the various economic indicators as guides in making investment decisions. In analyzing the indicators, you will find that some tend to *lead* business trends. For instance, a rise or fall in the number of *business failures* and of *new corporations* normally comes before a rise or fall in overall economic growth. New *building contracts* bring an encouraging outlook for certain industries—steel, building materials, construction. *New orders for durable goods* precede increased sales and earnings for the machinery, appliance, and auto industries. Frequently, investors make decisions on the basis of these indicators that seem to *lead* economic conditions.

Other indicators, such as *GNP* and *production indexes*, tend to *coincide* with or run alongside shifts in business conditions. These reflect changes in industrial activity. The end result comes out in reports of *corporate profits*. With profit-squeezing influences, such as high labor costs or inefficient operation, production and sales can increase while earnings go down.

Another group of indicators seems to *lag* behind trends in business activity. These include figures on *employment, disposable personal income,* and *consumer spending*. Figures on *retail sales* and *installment credit* also seem to follow other economic activity. Manufactures' *inventory accumulations* may indicate that business is falling off and that supply exceeds demand in certain products.

While economic indicators do offer a key in predicting business trends, you should use some caution in your interpretation of the indicators. First, they do not always move in the same direction at the same time—or at the same rate. Second, some economic forces bring long-term or lasting changes in business activities while others have only temporary influence. Last, specific industries and companies may show performance that runs counter to business trends reflected by economic indicators.

CHAPTER 4

✤ ✤ ✤

Sources of
Information

The information available on the world of business and finance is almost unlimited. It comes from a variety of sources beginning with your daily newspaper. Many veteran investors turn first to the financial pages of their paper to read the market reports. Here they learn the changes in the prices of stock traded on the exchanges each day as well as the opening, high, low, and closing prices. Other information on individual listings is given in the stock tables, including the amount of dividends declared, the dividend payment date, notice prior to the date that a stock goes "ex-dividend"—or without dividend. You will also learn which stocks were most active, the bid and offer quotes on stocks that were not traded, and transactions in bonds listed on the exchange. Most papers print daily stock tables for the NYSE and the American Stock Exchange, bid and ask quotations for the over-the-counter market, and transactions on regional exchanges.

Once you become an avid woman investor—usually after your first purchase of securities—you will find the financial pages in your newspaper even more interesting than the society pages and the sections on fashions, foods, and homemaking. You may be surprised by your own eagerness to get to the market reports each day to see what your money is doing.

General business news appearing in the financial sections of daily papers gives a running picture of economic activity and business trends. News items include figures on department-store sales, housing starts, bankruptcies, and production figures for key industries. You will also find a wealth of information on individual companies—mergers, new products, liquidations, price changes and managerial changes, developments in labor management relations, issues of new securities, stock splits, earnings reports.

Along with the financial news in your paper, you will find opinion columns written by financial columnists. These writers interpret economic happenings for the layman, present related background information, and analyze the financial news—past, present, and future. While these columnists are human and fallible, they do offer insights that many investors find helpful. Even the advertisements in the financial pages of a daily paper may offer information.

The general news sections in daily papers frequently include items of interest to investors and of financial significance. News influencing business activity includes *international developments* related to world trade, *election results* bringing different economic policies to government, *special legislation and regulations* related to business or agriculture, *actions of the Federal Reserve Board* affecting the money supply, *strikes or wage-hour agreements* bearing on prices and profits.

In addition to the daily newspaper, there are numerous other sources of investment information. Companies themselves provide firsthand information through annual reports, prospectuses, and special statements to stockholders. Personal contacts with those in management may also pay off in news of financial significance.

Firsthand business and financial news is available from business associations, labor organizations, state and local government, congressional reports, and various government agencies. Government bulletins are published regularly and made available to the public by the Internal Revenue

Service, the Department of Commerce, the Federal Trade Commission, the Interstate Commerce Commission, the Federal Reserve Board, the Securities and Exchange Commission, the National Labor Relations Board, Department of Labor, and the Council of Economic Advisers.

Specialized financial publications are excellent sources of investment news. Newspapers such as the *Wall Street Journal* and the *Journal of Commerce* specialize in business and finance news. The New York *Times,* while not just a financial publication, gives comprehensive coverage of financial news. Magazines in this field include *Business Week, Financial World, Dun's Review, Barron's, Forbes, The Exchange, Fortune.* Newsletters from many sources bring news reports and analyses. Some of the better known newsletters include *N.Y.S.E. Monthly Review, First National City Bank Monthly Letter,* the *Kiplinger Washington Letter,* and the *Federal Reserve Bank Monthly Review,* published by each of the 12 reserve districts.

If you are still looking for or are just beginning to build a file of investment information, a postcard or telephone call requesting material from brokerage firms, banks, and stock exchanges will bring you more than you can read. Other good sources of information include the Investment Company Institute, Standard & Poor's Corporation, Moody's Investors Service, Fitch Publishing Company, National Association of Securities Dealers.

For an overall approach and depth study of the investment world, you may want to read some of the following books on the subject.

GRAHAM, B. AND DODD, S.: *Security Analysis*, McGraw-Hill Book Company, New York, 1962.

GRAHAM, BENJAMIN: *Intelligent Investor*, Harper & Row, New York, 1965.

MERRITT, ROBERT: *Investing Today For Your Financial Future*, Simon and Schuster, Inc., New York, 1965.

SIMONS, G.: *What Every Woman Doesn't Know*, Macmillan Company, New York, 1964.

WILLIAMSON, ELLEN: *Wall Street Made Easy*, Doubleday & Company, Inc., Garden City, N. Y., 1965.

As you read up on the investment world and study the financial news, keep in mind that the information you find is only as reliable as its source. Try to get your facts from a source that has access to information, a reputation for accuracy and objectivity, and the ability to substantiate information. Look for recommendations and advice that are based on sound judgment and experience. When using the financial news as a guide in making investment decisions, be sure to evaluate information in terms of your own investment goals.

After buying your favorite paper towels, your favorite mayonnaise, your pet "anything," what fun (if you own some of the company shares) to look in the papers to see the impact your "huge" purchases have on your company's earnings. Joking aside—your financial reading needn't be dry if you make it a living matter. Money is created, spent, and administered by people. The whole world is a people-business. When you realize this and apply it to the business world, the financial pages can be fun!

CHAPTER 5

⚜ ⚜ ⚜

Your
Investment Goals

Although economics has been called the "dismal science," the business of stocks and bonds is not dry at all when you understand how business makes the world go round. Being an utter RR girl (and I am not talking about Rail Roads, rather the ludicrous ease of combining Romanticism and Realism), it is the romance of business and the people who devote themselves to it which stimulates my love for it. You too can be fascinated reading the annual report of any of the thousands of large and small corporations. Choose your industry—amusements, electricals, motors, textiles, electronics, oils, chemicals, steels. You will learn about people, places, and products. You will "sip a drop" of the stream we call capitalism—in its most productive aspect—creating jobs, raising our standard of living to a level unequaled by any other country in the world, developing marvelous new drugs, providing comforts and leisures never dreamed of by our parents.

How exciting while traveling on a plane to contemplate that by owning stock in the airline you own part of a bolt, a sliver of the fan of a jet engine, or the Kleenex container! What a romantic history—the birth, unfolding, blossoming, and mammoth development of the airline industry—backed by the aircraft industry which supplies the equipment. An ownership interest, i.e., common stock in any of these companies some 20 years ago, was for risk-taking accounts. This was for people with the means to take the risk involved—and it was for the person with vision and a sense of romance—for someone who could envision the explosion in air travel.

Even today just a small percentage of the population has been airborne. We have merely scratched the surface in air travel. The industry is galloping at a 20 percent annual gain. New technologies and techniques must be introduced to cope with this growth. As is true with *all* companies, the decisions of today make for progress or regression tomorrow.

Another example comes to mind! Remember the typing pools—scores of girls copying, copying, copying, copying? Suddenly machines—wet and dry process—made copies galore in a jiffy. No Utopia to be sure—many processes did not survive and investors in these companies did poorly. But there were glorious successes, too. Being in the right industry is not sufficient—it must be the right company in the right industry!

Our society is in a revolution in all its sciences, in all its services. Our society is in motion—mentally and physically. Managers who do not recognize this must fall by the wayside. The investor must make certain that the managers of the companies in which he owns a share are adept at combining the conservative and the progressive—men who plan for the future while they make the most of the present.

Before we tackle various instruments and choices of investment, we should realize the delicious position in which we find ourselves; i.e., to *have a choice*.

First, let's take a look at your investment goals— and then at the various instruments you can use to achieve them. People invest money for various reasons—most importantly to make their money grow. Security is top on the list of investment objectives for many people. Others like to invest for the sheer joy of seeing what wonderful things money can do.

Your investment goals will depend largely on your financial situation. Your primary objective may be long-term gains or capital appreciation if you are young and have years of earning ahead of you, or if you are married and have income of your own. You may also be willing to take certain risks if you inherit a large amount and do not need it for day-to-day living, or if your future is secured by a pension plan, a trust, insurance, or an annuity.

Investment goals will avoid much risk if you are a widow in middle or late years with a limited income, if you are a young widow with children to raise and a limited earning capacity, or if you are in your middle or late years with limited income and less than adequate provisions for your non-earning years. In these situations your primary investment goal will be income—regular and dependable. You will also be more concerned with safety and assurance that the full value of your principal will be returned to you.

Briefly—if you have already achieved substantial financial security and have extra money, or if you are young and your earning power is certain and largely ahead of you, you can afford to risk capital for the sake of long-term gains. On the other hand, if your current income is limited and not likely to increase, your investment decisions must be largely conservative to provide income and safety.

YOUR INVESTMENT GOALS ✣ ✣ ✣

Of course, any investment plan assumes that you have first established *basic* security with adequate savings and a reasonable insurance program. With this foundation, you are ready to approach the world of stocks and bonds.

Setting Investment Goals

The following personal and financial-planning sheet is almost self-explanatory. It is one way all the facts may be "put on the table" so that decisions can be based on the existing statistics and facts, as well as calculated planning. It brings out the need to satisfy requirements for protection. Many a time I sit down with young couples and find that they have no funds available for investment as yet because their insurance program is not adequate. Sufficient insurance and reserves have to be built up before you should assume the risks inherent in investing in stocks and bonds.

Setting investment goals is largely a matter of assessing your current financial position, deciding what you want to achieve, and devising a method for getting yourself *from* where you are *to* where you want to be. The "financial-planning information sheet" will get you through the first step in setting investment goals. It will also help you discuss your situation intelligently with your broker or financial advisor. This should result in your *method* or *plan* to enable you to reach your goals.

Know your primary goal and act accordingly. For instance, if the analysis of your circumstances shows the need for an emphasis on *income securities of high quality*—be of unwavering mind. Stick with this goal until a shift is indicated by your own changing conditions.

Keep in mind as you work with your financial advisor that anything you discuss will be treated as strictly confidential. Remember too that unless you confide in and provide necessary facts for your advisor, he cannot help you! It would be like asking your doctor to treat you without letting him examine you.

When you have filled out the planning form—or assembled information in a similar way—give serious thought to your investment goals. Each person has a different approach to investing just as each shopper winds up with different foods in her grocery basket. Don't let yourself be led by what someone else is doing. Your plan should be tailor-made —just for you. An example of such a form follows, reprinted through the courtesy of Vance, Sanders & Company, Inc.

YOUR INVESTMENT GOALS ⚜ ⚜ ⚜

PERSONAL DATA

1. Family Data:
   Marital Status: ....
   Children: Minor .... Adult ....
   Retired: Yes ☐ No ☐

2. Approximate annual income:
   Under $5,000 ☐ $5,000 to $15,000 ☐ $15,000 to $25,000 ☐
   $25,000 to $50,000 ☐ $50,000 and over ☐

3. Do you have a will? Yes ☐ No ☐
   Is property left outright to spouse? ☐
   Is property left through trusts to spouse? ☐

4. Is an inheritance anticipated?
   Yes ☐ No ☐
   If yes, amount.

5. Have living trusts been created?
   Yes ☐ No ☐

6. Have gift exemptions been used?
   Yes ☐ No ☐

7. Is financial support provided for relatives other than wife
   and children?
   Yes ☐ No ☐

8. Are bequests planned for favorite charity?
   Yes ☐ No ☐

FINANCIAL DATA

	Individual Ownership By Investor	Jointly Owned	Individual Ownership By Spouse
Fixed Dollar Assets:	$............	$............	$............
Bank Savings Accounts	....	....	....
Savings & Loan Accounts	....	....	....
U.S. Savings Bonds	....	....	....
Corporate Bonds	....	....	....
Municipal Bonds	....	....	....
Mortgages	....	....	....
Total Fixed Dollar Assets	....	....	....
Common Stocks (total) (Details on next page)	....	....	....
Mutual Funds	....	....	....
Real Estate (net of loans)	....	....	....
Business Interests	....	....	....
Life Insurance Cash Value	....	....	....
Total Assets	$............	$............	$............

Amount of Life Insurance Protection $..

YOUR INVESTMENT GOALS ❧ ❧ ❧

SECURITIES

No. of Shares	Name	Original Cost	Present Market Value
....	....	$..........................	$..........................
....	....	....	....
....	....	....	....
....	....	....	....
....	....	....	....
....	....	....	....
....	....	....	....
....	....	....	....
....	....	....	....
....	....	....	....
....	....	....	....
....	....	....	....
....	....	....	....
....	....	....	....
....	....	....	....
....	....	....	....
		$..........................	$..........................

Following the Path to Your Goals

There is a saying that applies *too* frequently to people in setting up an investment program. "You never plan to fail, but you often fail to plan!" When it comes to your financial planning, everything you do should have special meaning, an explanation, a thought-out tailor-made approach *for you*. There are questions you want to ask yourself, such as:

Do I invest or speculate according to my circumstances and ambitions? Do I think (without hoping for the "moon") that I can reach my objectives? In other words, are my goals obtainable?

Am I emotionally steady? Will I remain steadfast in carrying out my long-term program?

Do I know where to investigate, where and how to find reliable advice? Do I select all professionals I call on carefully—on the basis of facts and recommendations rather than emotional reaction?

Do I have a realistic concept of how much I know and am able to understand? I am not an engineer, architect, or geologist—it's better to admit it than to act "big" and make mistakes!

Do I know the basic rule of "not expecting too much too soon?"

The first thing to look for with the help of your financial advisor is the *quality* of the company. Examine its history in terms of dividend payments through various up-and-down economic periods—

through the "thick and thin" of the business cycle. There are good booklets with statistical facts along these lines. The New York Stock Exchange has a booklet entitled *Dividends Over the Years*. Investment firms have booklets with various titles describing and listing these types of securities.

I use an expression, "there are no bargains when the sun is shining," meaning that you pay a price for *popularity*. However, when an industry is basically sound but temporarily depressed—or in the shade so to speak for transitory reasons—there may be bargains. This has applied at times to various industries from motors to tobaccos to building to banking to utilities. To give a brief example—when interest rates are high the utility companies are "squeezed" since they have to raise funds at almost all times. This squeeze results in lower earnings, which normally remedies itself when money market conditions change. I am not implying that this will always remedy itself, but in the past it has done so. As a result, the tried, high-grade, old-line gas, water, and telephone company shares may be selling at lower prices when money is tight. However, since their earnings do not dip sharply, they usually can continue to pay the same dividend, and as a result the yield, or percent of return on investment, on these shares is higher. This presents an opportunity

TYPICAL SAMPLE PORTFOLIO
CAPITAL GAINS PLUS INCREASING INCOME

Most investments in common stocks are based on their potential for capital gains and prospects of increasing dividend income. Investors have been able to more than offset inflationary trends through well-selected common stocks. For example: Shares of a certain food company purchased in 1960 provided a return of 3.3 percent—but today the yield is equivalent to 5 percent in terms of original cost. The following companies have reported substantial earnings increases over the years, which have been reflected in higher dividend payments.

Shares	Companies	Price	Cost	Ind. Div.	Annual Income	Current Yield	Average* Price 1960	Yield on 1960 Purchase
200	Drug Company	$ 53	$10,600	$0.85	$ 170	1.6%	$13	6.5%
200	Food Company	48	9,600	1.60	320	3.3	32	5.0
100	Photographic Company	121	12,100	2.15	215	1.8	55	3.9
200	Department Store Co.	59	11,800	1.70	340	2.9	35	4.9
400	Utility Company	25	10,000	0.76	304	3.0	14	5.4
140	Oil Company	74	10,360	2.65	371	3.6	35	7.6
200	Television-Electronics Company	52	10,400	1.35	270	2.6	18	7.5
TOTAL			$74,860		$1,990	2.7%		

*Adjusted for subsequent stock splits and stock dividends.

for the income-seeking investor as well as for those seeking capital appreciation.

Sometimes other conditions can cause a temporary decline in earnings. If properly analyzed and investigated, such a situation—which might spell despair to the unsophisticated investor—could offer true opportunity to the sophisticated, well-informed and/or advised investor. For the knowledgeable and industrious there is never a period without opportunity of some sort. At times these opportunities may be more evident than at others, but they always exist.

The analysis of your circumstances may indicate an emphasis on growth-type securities which pay relatively little in dividends due to reinvesting of earnings to accomplish more rapid growth. If this is your need, be of the same unwavering mind. Stick with this goal until a revision is indicated by your own changing conditions! *Quality*, as with the income-type company, is of great importance if you are investing and not speculating. As you would check on past dividend payments in an income company, so you would also check for uninterrupted increases in earnings in a growth company. In fact, you will need very accurate figures of the annual growth rate over a period of some years. Many

TYPICAL SAMPLE PORTFOLIO
CAPITAL GAINS, GOOD QUALITY

This diversified portfolio consists of quality common stocks of well-established companies, important factors in their respective industries. They have experienced above-average growth in the past, and their future prospects look promising. The shares have appeal for prospective long-range capital appreciation.

Shares	Companies	Price	Cost	Ind. Div.	Annual Income	Yield
100	Metal Company	$ 76	$ 7,600	$1.60	$ 160	2.1%
100	Drug Company	82	8,200	2.10	210	2.6
250	Wire Company	30	7,500	1.00	250	3.3
300	Food Processing Company	27	8,100	0.80	240	3.0
200	Electrical Appliance Company	47	9,400	1.16	232	2.5
80	Electronics Company	106	8,480	0.60	48	0.6
TOTAL			$49,280		$1,140	2.3%

factors have to be checked currently and diligently to be sure no deterioration sets in.

The profit margin is one thing to look at closely. This is the percentage of sales brought down to profit. Has it improved from year to year with no more than occasional, temporary interruption? You also want to be sure that research and development outlays are keeping up. With most companies the lag between research and subsequent profits is a period of years. Any neglect of research could stunt the growth of the company—in fact it could cease to be a growth company altogether.

Management is another key factor—the agility, skill, and watchfulness of managing a growth company is prerequisite number one. The average age of those in command can be important. Are they endowed with sufficient experience and yet young, aggressive, and daring enough to accept the challenge of the future as pertains to the economy, their industry, their company?

For the most part, the compound theory applies here. The compound theory is merely letting the interest on money and interest on interest pile up like a snowball rolling downhill. So it is with any growth company which truly deserves this identification. Your earnings are earning, thereby com-

TYPICAL SAMPLE PORTFOLIO
LIBERAL INCOME

For many investors, income is the prime consideration. The following securities provide yields comparable to, or greater than, prevailing bank interest rates. These stocks also offer moderate appreciation potential over a period of time.

Shares	Companies	Price	Cost	Ind. Div.	Annual Income	Yield
200	Natural Gas Company	$41	$ 8,200	$1.80	$ 360	4.4%
400	Food Processing Company	21	8,400	1.00	400	4.8
600	Iron Ore Mining Company	12	7,200	0.80	480	6.7
250	Utility Company	32	8,000	1.52	380	4.8
130	Oil Company	64	8,320	3.30	429	5.2
200	Railroad Company	39	7,800	2.00	400	5.1
TOTAL			$47,920		$2,449	5.1%

pounding the investment you have in the company to an ever-increasing degree. Be sure the industry group you select is truly of the growth type. Generally speaking, a medium-sized company would be more likely to grow than the "already giant."

All the above merely demonstrates that following the path to your goals is not a simple matter. First, you must know your goals. Second, you must be steady and stick with them. Third, you must be certain that the vehicle you are using *is* truly suitable and remains suitable. This takes us right into the advisability of working with professionals.

Working with Professionals

Women are indeed a potent force in the economic life of our country. As discussed in Chapter 1, "Who is the Woman Investor?", women own close to half of the nation's entire wealth. They must now realize that obtaining and saving funds is no more important than maintaining them. As Thomas Aquinas once said, "The art of acquiring money is subordinate to the art of using it." Financial assets require "tender, loving, *intelligent* care."

Just as you need a doctor to look after your health —to examine you and prescribe medication when you are ill, so do you need professional help with your financial affairs. Unless you are unusually gifted—or just plain lucky—you will not be able to do without the services of the professional.

If your exposure to the business world has been limited you may require an advisor with greater than average patience—someone who can dispel your anxiety and fear of the unknown. You want someone who is quite obviously concerned about your problems—and who gives you that personal "cared-for" feeling. When you are seeking competent financial advice, look for a qualified person with integrity, training, skill, and knowledge. The professionals who can serve you well in this area include the broker, the investment counselor, the banker, the accountant, and the attorney. The particular functions and specialties of these experts are described in greater detail in Chapter 9, entitled "The Professionals Who Can Help."

Examples from Life

The following case histories bring alive the importance of *family* planning—the necessity for planning on the part of a young woman who thinks marriage and the husband's planning will relieve her of any responsibility; the need for a widow to be conservative when the temptation of a "fast buck" tempts her to speculate; the need to be equipped to think and plan on the part of a woman who may think that widowhood is years away!

There are ever so many more case histories which could be used to demonstrate the same points or related ones; however, there seems no need to elaborate the point which I am trying to stress on every page of this book. *Be willing to think, as a challenge before it is even a necessity; to find the proper guidance; to work with the "professionals" diligently; to follow the path to your goals as they are tailor-made by you and the professionals.*

Mr. X and "We"

Mr. X. is a charming, successful gent—he loves his wife, his family, his automobile, his suburban mansion, his golf club, his city club and all his other comforts and pleasures. Like many others, he is always wishing he could afford to live the way he lives!

Some days his overhead "load" weighs on him more than others. On one of these days, he visited my office. As we were chatting, he became more and more depressed over the futility of trying to plan ahead financially.

I dropped a little "bomb" by saying, "Have you ever discussed this with your wife?"

He said, "Why worry her?"

I replied, "Because she will be more worried when she is faced with the facts that the financial future is unplanned, bleak, and unsecured."

I sold my idea. "We" had a family session, and Mrs. X. took over the finances. "We" went without a few vacations. "We" didn't trade the car quite as often. "We" did without a few things.

But "we" enjoyed a great deal more because of planning and shared responsibility. It was just a matter of foregoing a few immediate pleasures for some important future goals and purposes.

Moral of the story: In cases where family sharing has not been a matter of course, try a financial "community plan." I have seen it work wonders— especially when financial clouds seem to be blowing up a storm.

Glamour Is Fleeting

The ex-beauty queen from Northwestern—just recently turned career girl. Will she marry? Just about any time she snaps her well-manicured fingers! Her fiance is a glamorous, young La Salle

Street attorney. How about her finances? She thinks buying conservatively has little in the way of kicks —I convince her to the contrary. Over a period of about 20 years, we accumulate for her odd lots of stock in fine-name companies selected for their "bargain" status at the time of purchase.

A twist to the story—glamor days vanish; marriage never materializes; family sickness eats up inheritances; personal sickness of a chronic nature befalls our girl. What is her financial lifesaver? The nest egg so "unglamorously" accumulated, so propitiously existing.

Moral of the story—make the savings count when you start. Lay the groundwork for security before you let wishful thinking guide your choices.

The Widow's "Might"

One morning the phone rings, as it does all day long. At the other end is a physician client of mine asking me to see one of his patients whose "illness," in his opinion, is due to the fact that she has been recently widowed and is completely at loose ends financially. My answer is "glad to" and an appointment results. After a complete financial checkup and many get-togethers, we arrive at a blueprint which enables her to live peacefully. Unless I tell her there is something to worry about, she won't!

We are retaining the securities in her husband's portfolio even though they do not bring enough of a return for her to live in the style to which she is accustomed. We decide that rather than sacrifice these capital-gains-oriented, proved securities, we would sell a few shares of stock each year to supplement her income. The years which followed were gratifying. The appreciation of assets justified retaining these securities—and the invasion of principal to supplement income was negligible.

Later my client, whose account did not allow for speculation, purchased an aircraft stock on March 3, 1965 at 39⅜—on her brother's advice. Upon my insistence, she sold these shares on August 24, 1965 at a net profit of about 7 points. Subsequently, the stock rose tremendously in value, causing her great regret about the "profit which might have been."

Later, however, after a series of adverse happenings resulted in the company passing the dividend in October of the next year, these shares dropped to 7 points below my client's original purchase price. Time bore out the fact that she has no business speculating where the risk of erratic movements and the possibility of uncertain dividends exist. Just because it was successful once did not make it *suitable* for her. It could just as easily have resulted in a loss —and she could not afford to assume that risk.

YOUR INVESTMENT GOALS ✤ ✤ ✤

Girl in the Audience

During one of my many speaking engagements, I met a most personable young woman in her 30's who, with her mother, attended a talk before a group of university women from a suburb near Chicago. As we talked, I discovered that the woman and her husband, a professional man, had never discussed any financial matters outside of running a household. They had no overall financial goals set up as a family; rather he was careful not to mention them.

This intelligent woman felt her lack of knowledge acutely. We had a most satisfactory talk—I convinced her that it was never too late to learn. This she began to do, checking with me from time to time to be sure that her reading and "boning up" were properly focused. She phoned me with much apology because she was not a client in the sense that she gave me business. However, she assured me that if she ever obtained funds and authority to act, I would be her broker. I assured her that there was personal satisfaction for me to know that my professional contact stimulated her to learn more about financial matters.

Little did we know that within less than a year her husband would pass away, leaving her with three children and modest means. She felt lost indeed—and resentful that her lack of preparation put her at such a disadvantage.

When she came to me, we worked hard—first, to find out just what we had to work with; second, where we should compromise—knowing the one thing which could not be compromised was quality. She needed all the security she could get. We decided to invest most of the insurance money in investment-company shares, selecting a fund with a portfolio of blue chip securities. We agreed that if there was no way she could live on her income, she would use a small amount of principal annually rather than aim toward high-risk, high-yielding but lesser-quality securities.

What do you think my "girl" did? Just what I thought—she found a part-time job which gave her the extra funds she needed. This was 10 years ago— now "we" are over the hump financially. The children are almost educated; my "girl" is still working because she loves it and the investment has done well for her. There are all kinds of morals in this story. To name a few: "It's never too late!"— "Never sacrifice quality!"—"You can't give up in despair!"—"Keep thinking!"

Getting Started—Keeping Up

Once I asked an Englishman how he managed to have such an outstanding lawn. It was a green carpet-like expanse—a vision to behold for anyone who has struggled with lawns as I have. He answered calmly, "All we have done is care for it religiously for a few hundred years." So it is with your investments—care is the answer, my friend! Whenever I look at a beautiful portfolio, it is like a fine jewel—an art treasure—a masterpiece—because it portrays the thinking, the caring, the constancy of its "master." So, to repeat the title of this section, "getting started, keeping up"; that is exactly the idea. Get the right start and don't ever stop.

Now, please, no tears if you have not been off to the right start. Recently I spoke to a new woman client who deplored her late start. I comforted her in projecting what could still be accomplished. To learn by the past and plan for the future is her new motto. Let it be yours too!

How do we get the right start? By forming the proper *tailor-made* investment objectives and determining a method of intelligent, vigilant pursuit of goals—the right ones.

CHAPTER 6

✤ ✤ ✤

Selecting the Proper Vehicle to Reach Your Goals

These are the Soaring Sixties—what a far cry from the days when the federal budget was no more than $8 billion. When was that? As short a time ago as the mid-thirties! Incomparable—and irreversible —changes have completely altered our economy over the past half century. In the early 1900's there was no Department of Commerce or Labor, no Federal Trade Commission, no Federal Reserve System— and no income tax! We are indeed in a different era and we owe it to ourselves to make the best of it.

Government expenditures such as defense spending, building of roads, schools, and other public welfare projects give government a way to stabilize employment and purchasing power—through tax changes, proper timing of expenditures, and automatically utilizing what economists have come to call "stabilizers."

Gross National Product increased from $103 billion in 1929 to approximately $740 billion in 1966. Total production of all goods and services much more than doubled in the past 12 years. Population increased by well over 50 percent—from 122 million in 1929 to 197 million in 1966. The number of persons engaged in production rose in roughly similar proportion.

The general price level declined in the great depression of the early 1930's; then came a partial recovery to a "plateau" only moderately above pre-1914. During World War II we had price controls which were effective for a time and later on yielded to the type of price inflation present during World War I.

What can we learn from our economic past? Is the long-term trend inflationary with intermittent periods of deflation? It would seem so. And during inflationary periods common stocks seem to do more for the investor than bonds or cash. Therefore it is difficult for the bond market to compete with the stock market as a hedge against inflation.

From all this, what can we learn about financial planning? What type of circumstances and conditions should we prepare for and guard against? We learn to know that a gamut of economic pros and cons can be translated into a "success story" only by means of an all-encompassing program. It requires a variety of financial instruments—fixed-dollar investments for safety and equity-type investments such as stocks to keep "current" in terms of purchasing power during times of inflation.

Stocks

Our first category, *the common stock*, represents ownership. Machinists, bakers, housewives, doctors, lawyers, nurses, bus drivers, schoolteachers—you name the category—may invest in a corporation via the stockholder route. One in every 10 persons, or approximately 20 million people in this country, is a shareholder! And over 10 million of them are women and girls. This type of equity interest is almost completely confined to democratic societies.

Why do people invest in stocks? Here are just a few reasons:

- To put children through college.
- To provide funds for a comfortable retirement.
- To obtain dividend income.
- To provide a hedge against inflation.
- To accumulate funds and provide financial security.

Common stocks represent ownership in a business. As part owner, you are entitled to a voice in the election of directors; you can vote on certain matters related to company operations; you share in profits or earnings—after prior obligations are met.

When you buy common stock in a company, you risk more and stand to gain more than the bondholder or preferred shareowner. The common shareowner receives no dividends until bond interest and preferred dividends are paid. However, when earnings are good, dividends on common stock tend to increase—this is not true of bond interest—and not usually true of preferred dividends. Common stocks are also more likely to grow or appreciate in value than are bonds or preferred stock. This makes them desirable as a hedge against inflation.

Preferred stocks do not normally offer the growth potential found in carefully selected common stocks. Rather they are noted for relative price stability. As far as risk goes, preferred stocks fall between common stocks and bonds. The preferred shareholder receives his dividends before common-stock shareholders. Preference to preferred stockholders also normally extends to proceeds received from the sale of assets should the company be liquidated. Generally, preferred dividends are limited to a specific rate—unless otherwise specified. (See the glossary for a description of various types of preferred stock —participating, cumulative, noncumulative, and convertible.)

When talking about common stocks, price movements are of the most interest and consequence. Despite the inherent difference in each company's stock price movement, there seems to be a strong tendency of *all* stocks to rise and fall together. This tendency of stocks to move in unison is particularly strong in periods of declining prices. Hence the commonly heard question, "What did the market do today?"

Factors influencing stock prices and the market as a whole are:

Profits—the immediate driving force behind stock prices. Anticipated higher profits should cause a rise in the price level while anticipated lower profits should cause a slump. For example, an anticipated increase in corporate taxes which, in turn, would decrease net profit, would be a bearish factor. An anticipated reduction in corporate taxes (such as we have had in the past by removal of excess profits taxes) would be a bullish factor.

Appraisal of price levels and business stability. For example, anticipated cutdowns in defense spending could spell overexpanded production. This could result in surplus supplies, unemployment, and a business slowdown. This in turn would lead to sliding price levels and should have an adverse effect on stock prices on the whole. On the other hand, increased demand and government orders such as those brought on by the Viet Nam conflict would make for a firming up in stock prices and possibly a substantial advance. At the same time, to the extent that a war—even a so-called "brushfire" conflict—disrupts the economy, causes dislocations, and shakes consumer confidence, the market may react negatively during hostilities.

Federal credit policy. Ample bank credit lends itself to potential business expansion, thereby creating an additional demand which may result in a rise in stock prices. Stringent credit policies could have the opposite effect.

In addition to major influences on the market generally, certain factors influence the prices of individual common stocks. Normally, individual stocks move with *cyclical swings of the general market.* If a particular stock goes completely against the market, i.e., if the market rises and a particular stock turns down or if the market turns down and the stock goes up, special factors are likely to be involved.

SELECTING THE VEHICLE ✤ ✤ ✤

News pertaining to a particular company can affect prices, too. For instance, you buy a good oil stock for income and appreciation. What sheer delight when you wake up one morning and read your morning paper at breakfast. You haven't quite rubbed the sleep out of your eyes when you see the headline in the papers. The financial page says *your* oil company has just discovered a huge new oil pool or ore deposit. This will make the stock go up, most likely; if later news brings disappointment as to the size of the deposit, or if time brings news that nothing will happen to add to earnings until 1995—this may prove to be a short-lived spurt in price. However, if the later facts are as glowing as the first announcement, you may be "on a good one," meaning you are getting more gain than you ever expected—and sooner.

Factors that can affect the price of individual stocks include newly found methods, products, resources, or "talent."

METHODS of merchandising, producing, or marketing which bring a significant increase in sales volume can increase the market value of a stock.

Finds in the way of RESOURCES—whether it be minerals or oils—will as a rule boost the market price of a stock; on the other hand, disappointment as to estimated resources in a particular mine or oil field could make for a depressed market price. Stocks frequently reflect findings of new resources.

> In the way of TALENT, it is hard to escape noticing that management is a major factor in any business, so it should not be surprising that the market reflects its quality.
>
> Where I talk about METHODS I should probably have talked about PRODUCTS as well. I am thinking of the example we have in the case of drug companies where the effectiveness of new drugs or flaws discovered can cause the stock to gyrate.

Changes in a company's capital structure, such as a stock split or a new issue frequently bring about a price change.

A *stock split* as a rule makes for a higher market —there are ever so many examples. Splitting a stock is somewhat like dividing an apple into sections—you do not get more apple, you simply have more sections. Supposing a stock with a market value of $50 splits two for one. The person previously owning one $50 share now owns two $25 shares— but the value is still $50 no matter how you "slice" it! However, there are some advantages. For instance, the dividend, which may have been $1 a share on the old shares, may now be raised to 55 cents. So there would be a 10 percent increase in income right away (2 x 55 cents = $1.10 or 10 percent) over the previous dividend of one dollar. Many companies will not split their stock unless they see fit to increase dividends.

SELECTING THE VEHICLE ⚜ ⚜ ⚜

The basic reason for a stock split is that investors seem to show a decided preference for stocks selling at around $30 and under. Therefore, a split bringing a stock down to this price range could stimulate trading and bring the stock price up. However, this is definitely not true when adverse conditions exist. Splitting stock is rather like "pushing a string" when market conditions or the company's own record are not satisfactory. A New York Stock Exchange study shows older, more successful companies' shares would be selling at ridiculously high prices per share had splits not taken place at various intervals.

Another factor not to be ignored in considering stock splits is that companies prefer widespread share ownership—it makes for an active market. If someone has *more* than 100 shares, he'd be more likely to sell some shares than if he had exactly 100 shares and would be left with an odd lot. (One hundred shares is usually considered a trading unit—any lesser number is called an odd lot.) So, via the stock split, share ownership in many cases is broadened. Widespread ownership is also desirable because shareowners often become loyal customers if "their" companies manufacture consumer products.

Stock splits, insofar as they create an ample

supply of outstanding stock, also tend to help keep price changes orderly and at a minimum. A larger number of buyers and sellers tends to minimize fluctuations. This is desirable for market stability.

From the investor's viewpoint, a stock split is desirable *if* dividends are increased and if the lower price level stimulates trading and brings the split price up.

New issues, depending upon the particular situation of a company, might mean different things—their effect on the market price could either be good or bad. If a company needs new equity capital, it might have a bullish effect. On the other hand, a new issue might just spell dilution of equity and lower profits per share. The market price might reflect this by declining.

Other news also will frequently result in price changes for a company's stock. An *anticipated merger* frequently affects the market price either way. Much depends upon the terms, the commercial impact of the merger, and the soundness of the companies involved. *Anticipated change in earnings* often affects market prices. A decline in expected earnings may jeopardize past dividend rates and would therefore tend to depress the market. Increased anticipated earnings should bring up the price level.

Dividend policies may also affect the price of stocks. A dividend is a payment made by the company to its stockholders on a pro-rata basis. On preferred stocks, this is usually a fixed amount. On common stocks, the amount will depend on the financial position of the company. Dividends are likely to go up when earnings are up—and exceptionally good earnings may result in an extra dividend payment. When earnings are down, there may be no dividend at all for common shareholders. Normally, dividends are paid in cash—but occasionally they will take the form of additional shares of stock—called a "stock dividend."

Growth-company dividends may be low or nonexistent because earnings are needed for expansion and improvements. However, the low dividend is compensated by capital appreciation—*if* the company really grows.

Companies are not required to pay dividends on common stock. Policies vary. Some pay the same amount every year or quarterly. Most companies which pay dividends declare them on a quarterly basis. Average dividends run approximately 3.5 to 4 percent. To determine the yield on stocks you own or plan to buy, divide the amount of dividends paid annually by the price of the stock. If a stock is priced at $50 per share and pays $2 in annual dividends, it yields 4 percent (2.00 ÷ 50 = .04).

Bonds

As a bondholder you are a creditor of the company issuing the bond. When you buy a bond you are entitled to regular interest payments of a specified amount and to repayment of your principal at a specified time. The bondholder's claim on earnings and assets ranks ahead of both preferred and common stockowners. If the company fails to meet these terms, the bondholder can resort to legal action—forcing foreclosure on mortgage bonds or receivership if bonds are debentures.

(See the glossary for a definition of different types of bonds—collateral trust bond, convertible bond, debenture, equipment trust certificate, guaranteed bond, income bond, mortgage bond, note, tax-exempt bond.)

Generally, bonds are the safest form of securities investment—depending, of course, on the credit standing of the issuing company, government, or municipality. Bonds are appraised according to quality by several rating agencies. The following symbols are used by Standard & Poor's Corporation to indicate the quality of bonds:

AAA — highest grade	B — speculative
AA — high grade	CCC — ⎰ outright
A — upper medium grade	CC — ⎱ speculations
BBB — medium grade (borderline between sound and speculative)	C — income bonds paying no interest
	DDD — ⎱ all show default with
	DD — ⎰ relatively little
BB — lower medium grade	D — ⎱ salvage value

The bonds of companies with high credit ratings are so well protected that you are almost sure to receive full payment of interest and principal. Bonds normally sell in denominations of $1,000. Price and interest fluctuations are related primarily to prevailing money rates. When credit is easy and interest rates are low, bonds are traded at high prices and offer low returns. When credit is restricted and interest rates go up, bonds become a more important source of credit. They sell at lower prices and offer higher yields.

Convertible securities typically refer to bonds or preferred stocks which can be exchanged at the option of the owner for common stocks of the issuing corporation. The conditions by which the exchange is made are carefully spelled out. In a sense, convertible securities offer the opportunity to have your cake and eat it too. They have the safety and relative price stability of the bond or preferred stock together with the provision for sharing profits and growth through converting to common stock—if this should become desirable.

Don't get excited—you do pay a premium for the advantage of conversion—how much or how little depends upon the value "in stock"—if it is very close to the value "in stock," the premium may be great; if it is quite remote it may be very little.

There are several questions to answer before you invest in convertible securities.

- What is the *conversion basis*—the number or price of common shares you will receive in exchange for the senior security? For instance, you may buy a convertible bond at par value—$1,000. The conversion basis may be stated in terms of quantity—25 common shares— making each share worth $40 ($1,000 ÷ 25 = 40). If the conversion basis is stated as a price—$40 a share —this shows that you will receive 25 shares per bond ($1,000 ÷ 40 = 25).

- Does the conversion privilege last until the maturity date or does it expire earlier?

- Is the convertible security callable? In other words, does the issuer have the right to redeem the security at a fixed price in advance or at such time as he designates? This could be disadvantageous for the investor—particularly if he paid more for the security than its stated redemption price.

The best way to buy a convertible security is first to evaluate it as a bond or preferred stock, considering all that is important in buying one of these. Then evaluate it as a common stock or equity investment, taking into account all that applies to common stock. Base your final decision on the combination of the two evaluations. This can be a difficult choice—so get the best advice you can find.

Investment Companies

A third way to invest is through an *investment company*—a company which uses its capital to invest in other companies. There are two principal types: the closed-end and the open-end or mutual fund. Shares in closed-end investment companies, some of which are listed on the New York Stock Exchange, are traded in the open market—that is, bought and sold like other stocks. Capitalization of these companies remains the same unless action is taken to change, which is seldom. The price of shares in closed-end investment companies is determined by buyers and sellers in the market. Open-end funds sell their own new shares to investors, stand ready to buy back their shares at their current value and are not listed. Open-end funds are so-called because their capitalization is not fixed; they issue more shares as people want them. The price of these shares is determined by the market value of the fund's portfolio of securities at the time of purchase —plus, in most cases, a sales charge.

A new—and interesting—type of closed-end fund is the dual fund. These funds have two classes of shares—income shares for those seeking current and future income, and capital shares for those seeking capital appreciation. The objective of these funds is to provide long-term growth of capital and income. From the investment of the capital furnished by both classes, the income shares receive all of the dividend income, while the capital shares receive the benefit of capital appreciation. Thus, each class of shareowners has the "leverage" of the investment of both classes working for its objective. After initial distribution, these shares are bought and sold in the same manner as the shares of closed-end investment companies.

Investment companies cannot and do not eliminate the inherent risk of investing; they simply *reduce* these risks through broad and selective diversification and continuous supervision of investments by highly skilled professional money managers.

In selecting an investment company, you need to appraise frankly your own particular objectives.

SELECTING THE VEHICLE ⚜ ⚜ ⚜

On this basis, you can choose those investment companies whose stated objectives and investment policies coincide with your own. Different investment companies have different objectives, including relatively generous current income, growth of principal and/or income, relative stability in principal and/or income, realization of capital gain, trading profits, or some combination of these. The best way to judge whether a fund meets your objectives is to study its past record. And, of course, discuss your goals with a qualified broker or financial adviser.

Mutual funds afford the investor, both large and small, an opportunity to share in the growth of America. They are not intended to make you rich overnight. The vast majority of mutual fund owners hold their shares for the long term—and this too helps reduce the risk involved. Time is on the side of the investor so long as the general direction of our economy is moving up.

There are funds tailored to almost any investment objective. Some funds include only stocks of certain industries in their portfolios; others restrict their holdings to bonds, convertible issues, or preferred stock; still others buy stocks of companies in a particular geographic area. Shopping for the right fund for you requires as much care—and professional guidance—as buying an individual security.

Under the law, a fund may not invest more than 5 percent of its assets in the securities of any one issuer, nor may it own more than 10 percent of any one issue. In practice, few funds would place so many eggs in one basket. After all, one of their main selling points is relative safety through diversification.

As with all business, management plays a vital role in the success of a fund. Good management seeks to maximize profits in a rising market and to cut losses in a declining market.

Again, I stress, get expert guidance in selecting the investment company best suited for your particular needs. And the best way I know to judge whether a fund meets your objectives is to determine whether or not it has in the past achieved these goals. Has a fund which seeks capital gains demonstrated that it has been able to achieve them in the past? Has a fund whose objective is income provided a good return on its investments in the past?

Judging things on past performance is a part of our daily life. We do this with the butcher, the TV repair man, our physician just about every day of our lives—and it's a philosophy well worth carrying over into the financial area. But in so doing, it is important to bear in mind that all investments are subject to market fluctuations. Thus, the past results of a fund should not be considered as a representation of future performance, but rather as a guide to how the fund has fared under market conditions in prior years.

Investment companies have programs for investing sums of money at regular intervals and reinvestment of dividends and/or capital gains for the accumulation of additional shares. Plans may provide for the custody of these shares by a bank which sends out regular notices to show status as to number of shares, etc. Programs may usually be discontinued at any time without penalty. However, some contractual plans call for the greatest share of sales commissions to be paid during the first two years. In this case, buyers may suffer a penalty by discontinuing the plan in a short period of time.

These plans enable investors to invest sums of money systematically and conveniently and also follow the principle known as "dollar-cost averaging" (see page 107), which means investing equal amounts of money at regular intervals over a period of time; thereby you acquire more shares at low prices and fewer shares at high prices.

Because systematic accumulation plans cannot

protect against loss in value in declining markets, an investor should consider his financial ability to continue purchasing shares through periods of low price levels. If a plan is discontinued when the market value of the accumulated shares is less than the cost, the investor will incur a loss.

This method of systematically accumulating fund shares, however, is designed to level off the peaks and valleys of price fluctuations and to produce an advantageous average cost in relation to long-term market trends.

The usual brokerage commissions are charged generally for the purchase and sale of closed-end funds. In the case of mutual funds, a certain percentage of the fund's asset value is charged to buy shares. This charge is included in the offering price, and depending on the fund and the amount of money you invest, ranges to a maximum of about 8.5 percent. Naturally, the larger your investment, the lower this percentage will be. Normally, there is no charge for redeeming your shares. In addition, there are some funds, known as "no load funds," which operate without a sales charge.

All investment companies—both closed and open-end—naturally have operating expenses. These consist of the management fee—what the shareholders pay the fund's managers for their professional guidance—legal fees, bank custodial fees, and other overhead. These charges average about seven-tenths of one percent of the fund's assets and are deducted from the annual income earned before distribution to shareholders in the form of dividends.

The performance of investment companies depends on the type of fund. Balanced funds are designed to resist market slides because of holdings of bonds and preferred stocks. Growth funds, because their portfolios include common stocks of a venturesome nature, generally decline in a bear market— and go up in a rising market.

The major advantages of the investment-company route to stock ownership are professional management of your money and diversification which reduces risk. These two advantages can be of particular importance to small investors with limited funds which do not permit diversification. The small investor may also find it difficult to get the professional advice and management services which are readily available to those investing large amounts. One of my clients went to a luncheon at which her lady friends were discussing their various investments—with much pride and delight reflecting upon their affluence. My client, who has a small income which she receives from investment company shares, played a nice joke. After each high-grade security mentioned, she said, "I have it!" Finally, one of the "girls" spoke up and asked, "How can you possibly own that much?" My client calmly replied, "I own mutual fund shares and they have it in their portfolio, so—that means I own it!"

Before buying be sure that a mutual or closed-end fund is the right form of investment for you—and be sure you find the company that has in the past most consistently come closest to satisfying *your* investment goals.

CHAPTER 7

Making Sense of Wall Street's Jargon

By now you are no stranger to the business world. You know how the economy works. You understand the fundamentals of the securities market. You know what types of securities best fit your investment goals. When most women reach this point in their economic education, they are so romantically and financially involved in the business of stocks and bonds that they want to learn all there is to know. And that can be a lifelong project, a full-time hobby, a consuming interest. Every day brings a thousand new developments. To really be up on what's going on you need to know some of the terms used by investors and to understand a few theories of investing.

Professionals use special terms to describe stock-market trends and well-known methods of investing. You will see these terms regularly in brokerage firm market letters, financial periodicals, and newspapers. It's a good idea to understand them if for no other reason than to know what your money is doing.

Several key phrases describe market trends. A *bull market* is a long upward trend in stock prices, while a *bear market* is just the opposite—a prolonged decline. Prices of individual stocks may run counter to prevailing upward or downward movements. When the market is described as *sidewise*, it means there is no clear bull or bear trend. *Intermediate price movements* may occur within a bull or bear trend. *"Corrections"* or *"reactions"* are declines running counter to a major upward trend. *"Rallies"* are advances during a major downward trend. *Consolidations* and *building a base* refer to leveling-off periods when prices tend to stabilize before proceeding on a specific trend. *Seasonal market movements,* lasting about a month, occur within intermediate trends. *Short-term movements* occur weekly or daily.

In addition to being familiar with basic market terminology* you may want to understand some common investment theories and techniques. The experts have devised patterns to follow in analyzing

---

*For the complete "Language of Investing" see the Glossary.

and buying securities. This chapter will not make you a professional market analyst—but it will help you to make investment decisions more intelligently . . . to converse more effectively with your broker and other experts . . . to form a broad base of investment information.

Some professionals recommend *market-forecasting methods* of investing. There are two ways to forecast price movements—the *value approach* and *chart-reading.* The purpose of the *value approach* is to estimate a reasonable current price or value, in relation to possible *future quotations* of an issue. To estimate *value* the professionals consider projections of *earnings per share.* The projections are based on past, current, and prospective records of a company's growth, stability or decline in net profits, of dividend policy and record, of the financial condition in terms of assets and capitalization. In analyzing, the experts also look into product development, research activities, and plant expansion. They appraise the quality of a company's management. They assess the company's position in its industry, long-term industry trends, and general business and political influences.

The next step in valuing a stock is to consider projected *price-earnings ratios,* which are based on past and present *price-earning ratios* of the company and the industry, on the company's prospective earnings and dividends, and on dividend yields compared with stocks of similar quality as well as with bond yields and interest rates.

Finally the experts multiply the *earnings-per-share projection* by the projected *price-earnings ratio* to find the *value* or estimated reasonable price of an issue. The *value* may be above, below, or close to the actual market price. A stock may be a good choice if it sells at less than the *value*.

Those in favor of the *value approach* contend that it is based on realistic projections of factors which are likely to determine the future market price of an issue. Those opposed or unimpressed by the value approach say that *investor sentiment* tends to have a greater influence on market price. Hence *value* cannot be considered a sure key to future quotations.

Chart-reading is another method of anticipating stock prices. Charts record past and current price movements for individual stocks, for a combined group of stocks or a particular industry, and for the market in general. To interpret chart trends, market "technicians" emphasize (1) *resistance levels* which mark the highest price securities reach before going down again, (2) *support levels* which mark the lowest price securities reach before going up again, and (3) *price movements through these levels* which indicate bullish or bearish trends and provide buy or sell signals for investors.

Those who favor chart-reading say that it eliminates wild guessing in that recorded market action mirrors the attitudes of investors. Thus it offers a basis for forecasting. Others say chart-reading is unscientific—its assumptions haven't proved consistent with results. No one can forecast investor psychology and how it will influence the market.

In addition to market forecasting, specialists also rely on certain technical theories to make investment decisions. One theory is based on *market averages*. Daily price movements of selected issues are reflected by well-known averages such as the Dow-Jones Industrial Stock Average, Standard & Poor's 425 Industrials, New York Stock Exchange, and the New York *Times* Industrial Stock Average. Those who trade on market averages sell their holdings in a *bull market* if a specific *stock average* dips a certain percentage on an *intermediate reaction*. If the *average* moves up, the selling point goes up by the same percentage. They buy stocks in a *bear market* if the *average* moves up a certain percentage

during an *intermediate rally*. The buying point goes
down by the set percentage if the *average* continues
to decline. Trading on averages makes it easier to
maximize and cut losses. However, it is difficult to
know where to set buy and sell points. Also, individual stocks often do not move with the averages.

The *Dow Theory* is another guide to investment
decisions. Dow theorists generally look for large
daily movements in the average and increasing
volume for definite indications of a primary trend.
According to this theory, you can predict a bull
market trend when an *intermediate dip* in the Dow-
Jones Industrial Average stops before reaching the
low point of the *preceding intermediate decline*. You
can confirm this trend when the next *intermediate
rise* in the average is above the high of the earlier
rise. The bull market lasts as long as these conditions recur.

On the other hand, you can foresee a *bear market*
trend when an *intermediate high point* moves below
the top of the previous *intermediate rise*—it is con-
firmed when the next *intermediate dip* moves below
the low point of the previous decline. The bear market continues as long as these conditions recur.

Ideally, those following the Dow Theory would
buy stocks near the low point in a bear trend and

sell near the high mark in a bull trend. The Dow Theory does offer carefully figured timing for investment decisions. However, there may be a long lag between buy and sell signals. It may also be difficult to know for sure when the high point or low point has been reached.

The *Odd Lot Theory* is used by some investors in making decisions. The idea here is that small investors or odd-lotters trading in less than round lots frequently make mistakes about turns in the market. Therefore, if odd-lotters switch to selling in a declining market, this often indicates the bottom of the slide. On the other hand if odd-lotters buy heavily in a rising market, this frequently indicates that the market may be near the top.

For those who prefer to be systematic about investing, there are two common methods—*dollar-cost averaging,* a term you may have already heard about, and *formula timing plans. Dollar-cost averaging* involves investing a fixed amount of money at regular intervals over a long period of time—regardless of prices at the time of purchase. In other words, you buy $40 worth of a given stock every month. When the stock is selling at a high price, you get fewer shares than when it is selling at a low price. This permits you to benefit from price dips

provided the overall movement of the stock is upward. Of course you must select a stock that will
ultimately go up *and* have the will power to keep
buying it when the price is declining.

Suppose you decide to invest approximately $100
per month in shares of AB Corporation. To do this
on a dollar cost averaging basis your purchases
might run as follows:

Price of Shares		Number of Shares	Cost
$10.00	x	10	$100.00
5.00	x	20	100.00
2.50	x	40	100.00
5.00	x	20	100.00
10.00	x	10	100.00
		100	$500.00

Your average cost per share comes to $5.00 ($500 ÷ 100).

In several *formula-timing plans* changes in market prices serve as the primary guide to making investment decisions. Under the *constant-dollar plan*
you keep a specific amount of money invested at all
times in common stocks. When stock prices go up
you sell enough securities to bring the total value
of your investments down to the amount set. If

prices go down you buy enough securities to bring the total value of your investments up to that amount.

Under the *constant-ratio plan* you put a certain percentage of your investment dollars in common stocks and the rest in savings or other types of securities. As stock prices change you buy or sell to maintain the common-stock percentage.

The *variable-ratio plan* calls for decisions based partly on one of the well-known stock-market average. You vary the proportion of common stock to cash or other securities in your portfolio in accordance with the movement of a stock average. Usually you buy stock when the average goes down a set amount and sell when it rises by the same amount. Following this procedure your common-stock holdings should be light at the top of upward price movements and heavy at the bottom of downward movements.

While formula-timing plans help you avoid emotion and guesswork in making portfolio decisions, they also require considerable will power. In following these plans you may sell stocks which could offer further profits as well as a hedge against inflation.

Some investors consider *timing* a key factor in making a profit on securities. Buying and selling opportunities vary at different times of the year. In January and in midsummer months stock prices may go up as investors anticipate the usual spring and fall business pickups. March and April, along with November and December, may offer good buying opportunities resulting from tax considerations. In the spring investors frequently sell securities in order to pay taxes. Toward the end of the year switching and selling for tax reasons are common.

None of the investment theories and techniques discussed are perfect—and no one method of buying securities is right for everyone. You will undoubtedly want to work out an investment plan to meet your objectives with the help of your broker and the financial information available to you. Be sure to keep your individual investment goals in mind and to review your portfolio periodically.

Analysis of Different Industries

Large investment-counseling firms, brokerage houses, banks, and various other financial institutions which base decisions for themselves and/or their clients on research, employ analysts to cover various industries. This is because every industry has its own characteristics requiring specialized knowledge and experience. Comparing a utility and

110

a steel company, just to cite an example, is like comparing apples and bananas.

The following represents a simplified discussion of some of the basic factors affecting investment analysis of six key industries. The purpose of this section is to illustrate some of the diverse economic considerations with which we must reckon in examining various industries and companies.

Utilities. These are the companies which provide our electric, gas, water, and telephone services. As is true in some other industries such as airlines and rails, the rates charged are regulated by government agencies. In the case of utilities, the agencies are the Federal Communications Commission, Federal Power Commission, and the various state agencies. These rates are usually based on the company's investment in its plant, meaning buildings and equipment. In other words, the company is allowed to earn a set percentage, after taxes, of its investment in its plant. Moreover, regulation varies considerably from one state to another. Consequently, one of the most important factors to know about a utility company is the "regulatory atmosphere" of the state in which it operates.

Also, to evaluate the stability of a company's income, it is advisable to know how much of its revenue is derived from *residential, commercial,* and *industrial* customers. The more residential the better —people are not about to shut off the kitchen lights or turn off the phone because times are less affluent. Commercial and industrial activity, on the other hand, can be much more sensitive to the economy.

To prepare for future growth, utilities are required to raise large amounts of capital—mostly bonds—for their construction expenditures. As a result, changes in interest rates have some impact on the growth of common share earnings.

Utilities can and have satisfied *income* and *growth* needs of the investor. Much depends upon the particular area in which they operate. It stands to reason that in rapid-growth territory such as Florida, there would be a growth aspect to utilities stock in excess of other states. The price evaluation would most likely reflect this; i.e., it would sell at a higher price-earnings ratio.

Other factors affecting earnings include operating cost trends, tax rates, competition among various types of energy (e.g., electricity, gas, oil), and the development of new appliances.

An air of stability based on past performance generally surrounds the higher-grade utilities as a group. Gains in sales and revenues of the utility industry over the foreseeable future are indicated and periodic dividend increases can be expected.

Autos. Total auto demand equals normal replacement needs plus new purchasers. Over the past 15 years, the number of passenger cars in use in this country has grown by more than two-million units a year. It is now estimated that normal annual replacement demand is in excess of six-million units, or about two-thirds of the present estimated nine-million normal car year.

Growth in the industry comes from three areas: (1) a growing population, (2) the increase in multi-car families (owning two or more cars) and (3) the rising percentage of families owning a car.

In addition to the nearly 300,000-unit projected annual growth in demand, the industry will benefit from the long-term trend of "more car per car." Not only is the demand for special purpose cars growing, but our affluent society is enabling more and more buyers to satisfy their desires for more optional equipment. For example, more than one-third of all U.S. cars produced are air conditioned.

While the long-term demand for automobiles has followed the increase in disposable income, the industry is subject to cyclical fluctuations. The automobile is durable goods and if the consumer is not optimistic over business conditions, he can postpone replacing his car.

Imports have become a new factor in the domestic industry in the past decade and sales are now around the 700,000-unit level. The domestic manufacturers share in this market through imports of their own models made in their foreign manufacturing plants. In addition, all the major companies have substantial manufacturing and marketing facilities abroad and thus they are sharing in growth of the market outside the U.S. which is at a more rapid unit rate than is occurring domestically.

The factors which have resulted in the industry's moderate long-term growth can be projected well into the future. Therefore, subject to considerable fluctuations from time to time, the industry can look forward to increasing demand at least as great as in the general economy.

Oils. The petroleum industry certainly qualifies as a growth industry. Demand for oil and natural gas has increased each year since 1956 when worldwide consumption totaled 17 million barrels a day. In 1966, the total was 33.5 million barrels, a gain of nearly 100 percent.

A number of factors are working in favor of sustaining the industry's growth. One is population. The U.S. alone should show a population increase of 35 percent by 1985 to 265 million people. Demand for heating is expected to increase commensurately.

Another factor is the worldwide automobile explosion. Worldwide registration of vehicles increased 63 percent in the past 10 years, and the growth rate was even more dramatic in the past five years during which the total rose to 177 million from 138 million.

Statistics are not available for aircraft and boat registrations, but anyone who has experienced the delays in landing and take-offs which have become common at major airports is aware of the expansion of commercial air traffic. And the bigger the jets, the more fuel they consume. Today's 707 jet uses up 2.5 to 3 million barrels over its lifetime. The supersonic transports of the 1970's will require an estimated 30 to 40 million barrels—equal to a reasonably good-sized oil field.

The problem the industry faces is this—can it find adequate reserves to meet this demand? Oil officials concede it will be a difficult task, but they believe they can do it. They say they can achieve their goal by exploring in new areas—such as the continental shelves around the world. Production from tar sands, oil shales and even coal will be exploited, and new technology will be brought to bear.

A growth area within the industry is that of petrochemicals, with the demand for these products growing at a rate of three and a half times the national industrial average. Petrochemicals are derived by converting liquids and gases into a solid state. They are known by a bewildering array of technical names. In fact, there are some 10,000 different petroleum chemicals whose end-products are familiar household names—nylon, Dacron, Orlon, Acrilan, to cite just a few—everything from fibers and films to rubber and fertilizers.

Diversification has become almost a "way-of-life" with many companies. Accordingly, analysis of individual companies is increasingly complex. Almost all companies—large and small are now involved in foreign operation. The integrated companies, i.e., those that explore, produce, refine and market, are more stable investments since one segment often provides a hedge against another segment of the business. Normally earnings of companies in this category are capitalized by "the market" at 10 to 15 times. In contrast, earnings of "pure" producing companies are capitalized somewhat higher, often

15 to 23 times, since these companies are in the greater profit segment of the business and not exposed to the downstream operation (refining and marketing) which has large capital requirements, lower margins and greater inherent risks.

Chemicals. The chemical industry can be designated as a major growth industry—but selectivity is essential for the stock buyer. Competition is intense, and growth may be explosive, moderate, or negligible, depending on what company is selected. This competition in chemicals is not only national—it is international as well.

There are a multitude of products such as "heavy chemicals," plastics, synthetic fibers, agricultural products, industrial gases, exotic fuels. A "first" in any one of these categories may demand full prices. However, when competition sets in, as it did in the synthetic fiber and plastics areas, undercutting of prices may make it imperative to operate with exceptional efficiency in order to exist profitably.

In this industry, new products often render existent machinery and equipment almost worthless and completely new facilities are required. This explains why chemical companies are rather "notorious" for retaining a major part of earnings for new plant and equipment requirements, expansion, and modernization. Outlays for research also are heavy. In fact, while the ratio of spending on research to sales runs at about 1 percent for industry as a whole, it is about 3 to 5 percent for the chemical companies—recently, that is.

The high level of business activity continues to aid chemical sales. However, product mix—the variety and proportion of products—is very important. As mentioned before, companies in the synthetic fiber and plastics areas face severe competition which in many cases affects prices adversely. On the other side of the coin, sulphur prices until recently discouraged exploration; more recently, growth of fertilizer usages brought a rise in sulphur consumption, and subsequent higher prices.

This is strictly *my own* analysis from observation: chemical products tend to go through three major stages—the *pioneer* stage in which profit is often lucrative; the *mature* stage in which profit is adequate; the *oversupply* stage in which profit becomes a dilemma.

All this only highlights more acutely my opening remarks—selectivity of the company is the prime concern.

Steels. The steel industry gives us a variety of products for industry and home—from bridges to razor blades, airplanes and automobiles to washing machines and driers. In long perspective, uses of "light" steels such as sheet and strip have increased, thanks to the vigorous growth of our auto, appliance and container industries. These and other light steel markets now account for nearly half of the steel consumption.

However, uses of "heavy" steels such as plate and structurals still bulk large in the total picture. Construction, railroads and machinery can account for as much as one-third of the total in heavy capital spending years. Thus, the cyclical character of the steel industry—although less extreme than in the past—is still pretty much with us and probably will continue so in the foreseeable future.

Competition is plentiful within the steel industry. Foreign imports and substitute materials such as aluminum, plastics and concrete continue to chip away at steel's markets. This makes it imperative for steel companies to spend billions to improve product quality and cut production costs. Solid gains in efficiency and somewhat lower unit costs have already been achieved since the early 1960's when steel's technological revolution—somewhat belatedly —began to gather momentum in this country. Record spending continues—estimated at the $2.4

billion level in 1967, up from $2 billion last year. This rather than higher tariff barriers, leading steel-makers admit, would seem to give the only promise of winning the competitive race sometime in the future.

Implementing price increases on steel products has been somewhat difficult in the past. Steel is the most widely used metal—about 100 million tons annually as against only five million tons for aluminum, its nearest competitor. In the opinion of many, including government officials, steel prices influence most other prices. Hence, in their efforts to fight inflation, government price-cost watchdogs rarely failed to crack down on the steel industry in the past whenever a new price hike was attempted. However, the situation may be changing.

A "handful" of companies represent close to three-fourths of the industry's production. The so-called "integrated" companies mine the ore, refine it in furnaces, manufacture the sheet strip plate, pipe and structural forms and distribute the products. The "specialty" companies manufacture alloy steels for uses in tools, dies and the sophisticated machinery of the space age. The most widely known alloy is, of course, stainless steel.

Be it "integrated" or "specialty," it is difficult

for any newcomer to start producing steel for the simple reason that a large capital investment is necessary. One must be prepared to spend a dollar to get back a dollar in annual sales—which is two-to-three times higher than in many other industries. And only six or seven cents of the dollar will be retained as net profit—in a good steel year. Consequently, steel has what is sometimes called "cost-leverage"—the ability to show spectacular profit increases from a poor year to a good year.

The basic factor making all the difference between a good and a bad year for steel is "volume." Steel is a volume industry. When shipments go down profit margins shrink and vice versa. Very few steel companies can buck the trend and show improved earnings when the economy in general is in a downswing and the volume of shipments on the decline.

Nevertheless, steel equities stand out in two respects: 1) Normally, the yields on steel dividends are high—recently on the better side of 5 percent; and 2) Steel stock prices tend to fluctuate in close harmony with the general economic cycle, so that regularly opportunities for moderate speculation are created. Buying steel stocks when the time is "right" and selling them remorselessly in a strong market should in many cases prove quite rewarding.

121

By the same token, steel stocks are not suitable for investors emphasizing long-term growth, and peace of mind. Too many factors—continually high capital requirements, foreign competition—still affect the steel industry and steel equities will probably continue to have difficulties to make the "investment grade" for quite some time.

Electronic and Electrical Equipment. The electronic and electrical equipment industry is an amazing one indeed. Amazing in its capacity to give birth to new companies—amazing in the capacity of companies to produce products which revolutionize our lives industrially and personally. Within a decade, TV has become a household "necessity"—and we are transmitting "live" pictures of the moon.

The key word is growth, but great risks exist. Therefore, it is essential for safety to choose companies which have a good product mix and do not depend upon one product for profit. The industry is not the perfect basket for all eggs. It serves three major markets—consumer, industrial, and government. Consumer products are feverishly in demand at times, such as the craze for color TV. Industry products encompass such items as computers, nuclear power plants, power-plant equipment generally, and instrumentation and control devices. The industry is particularly sensitive to world political developments. A great many products are accentuated by war needs; still others flourish under peacetime conditions.

There are several specific things to look for in viewing a company in the electronic industry. First, the *size of the company's primary market*. When color TV sets are in demand, it is important to analyze the size of the potential market as accurately as possible when appraising a company for which this is the major product. This is true for any company whatever its market—washing machines, dryers, computers, generators, etc.

It is also important to take a look at the *quality and stability of management* in analyzing a company in this industry—particularly if the company is a "miracle boy, overnight wonder." *Research and development* are key factors in future earnings of the company. *Financial strength* is all-important for survival in the face of rapid changes, and for the flexibility which is essential in the electronic field. *Military contracts* should also be scrutinized carefully in those companies which are heavily dependent on defense business.

While some electrical companies consistently have yielded 5 percent or more, most firms in the industry pay a modest dividend or none at all. In lieu of cash, some companies pay stock dividends. These conservative dividend policies are common because the industry's rapid growth rate requires large amounts of working capital.

Equipment can be rendered obsolete quickly, so outlays for equipment may be large. Research is essential and intense—therefore large as a percentage of sales. For most investors, it would be wise to concentrate on companies in a number of markets—perhaps even in areas other than electronics and electrical—to be somewhat protected against demand changes. Key words for investing in this industry are care, selection, and a conservative approach. Happy surprises can still be possible with this attitude and calamities may be avoided. Risks can be way above average in companies not seasoned or tested; glamor and paying for hopes and expectations can be very expensive. I can only emphasize, find the best expert you can and let him take you by the hand.

This industry breakdown is an oversimplification if ever there was one. But it does demonstrate, even if oversimplified, that no industry is so foolproof as to provide the perfect basket for all your eggs. The key word is always diversification.

Understanding Risks

Before going any further with your investment plans it is essential fully to understand the concept of *risk*—the various types and degree of risk involved in buying and selling securities—even the risk of not risking your money in the market. Risk, in the stock and bond world, is the possibility of losing some or all of the money you've invested.

While it is possible to lose money on *any* investment, the potential gains outweigh risks for the investor who exerts a reasonable amount of caution and intelligence in selecting securities. Consider the facts. We live in a growing, dynamic economy. In 1966 our gross national product (national output or value of all goods and services produced in a given year) totaled over $740 billion. This was produced and consumed by a population of nearly 197 million. Compare that to a GNP of approximately 285 billion in 1950 when the population was 152 million. While population increased only 30 percent, GNP increased over 160 percent. By 1975 the economy will have to produce goods and services for an estimated population of over 215 million—a fairly certain sign of continuing economic growth and expansion.

Moreover, historical records of the securities market are encouraging. Of the 1247 common stocks listed on the New York Stock Exchange, over 789 can claim an uninterrupted *annual* dividend record for the last 20 years—regardless of market conditions. Over 560 of these companies have paid *quarterly* cash dividends for 20 years or more. Since 1930 the companies with stocks listed on the Big Board increased from 855 to over 1280; during the same period the market value of listed securities jumped from $49 billion to $483 billion.

The increasing number of individual investors is another indication of confidence in the economy. Today over 20 million Americans—one out of every six adults—own shares in publicly held corporations. Shareholders have more than tripled since 1952. Over half of adult shareholders are women. Over half of the individual investors have annual incomes of less than $10,000. In addition to individual holders, millions of people share indirectly in the ownership of American business by investing their money in savings banks, insurance companies, p e n s i o n funds, and other financial institutions which in turn buy securities.

Despite short-lived recessions and ups and downs in the market, the prospects for the future and the pace of the nation's business and industrial expansion point toward a continuation of overall economic growth. There are risks involved in buying securities, of course. But you can minimize possible losses when you understand types and degrees of risk—including market, company, industry, and economic.

Market risks are based on fluctuations in the prices of securities—the price may be down when you want to convert a particular holding to cash. These fluctuations depend largely on the supply of and demand for a security at a given time. When sellers outnumber buyers of a particular security the price drops. The psychological mood of the investing public also affects prices—when pessimism prevails prices tend to decline.

Company risks are based on conditions within a company. Such risks are largely the result of poor management and the inability of a company to compete successfully with other businesses in the same industry. You can minimize this type of risk by comparing financial reports of different companies and knowing what to look for before buying a security. The next section explains how to evaluate a company.

Industry risks are confined to individual industry groups. A variety of factors can affect the growth or decline of a particular industry. *Technological advances* within an industry can increase production and reduce operating costs, giving that industry an advantage. Lack of technological progress can create risks within an industry. *Product development or innovations in the use of materials* can influence the risk factor in an industry. For instance an increase in the use of aluminum may affect the sale of steel. *Consumer spending power* can have a serious impact on industries that manufacture consumer goods. The price of tobacco stocks fell sharply after the Surgeon General's report of 1963. *Government spending* also contributes to the growth or decline of certain industries. War or threat of war increases spending for defense and raw materials, which is good for some industries. The Education Act of 1965 increased the demand for educational materials, visual aids, textbooks, and school facilities and equipment.

Overall economic risks grow out of the fact that the growth rate of our economy varies from year to year—we have alternating periods of boom and recession. To minimize general economic risks:

- Invest in sound, established industries such as utilities for reasonable safety and relatively stable income.

- Trade in cyclical industries for short-term profits.

- Remember that not all segments of the economy are equally affected by market trends.

- Hold onto solid investments regardless of market trends
  —provided you can anticipate long-term growth.

Speaking of economic risks, inflationary trends can make it a greater risk to save money than to invest it. The long-term decline in the purchasing power of the dollar will reduce the value of savings while money put in common stock may increase in value with the growth of the economy—unless investments have been largely speculative.

While not wishing to gloss over the risks involved in buying securities, I want to emphasize the fact that investing in American business is one of the best-known ways to make your money grow, provide for financial security, and build an estate. A recent study, *Economic Behavior of the Affluent*, shows that the rich make a good part of their money in the market. This survey, conducted by three economists from the University of Michigan, was based on close to 1,000 interviews with persons having annual incomes ranging from $10,000 to over $1 million. According to the study, those in upper-income groups are well-informed investors—avid readers of business and financial publications. They invest heavily in common stocks. These people attribute their wealth almost entirely to appreciation of assets. Moral of the report: Calculated risks pay off.

CHAPTER 8

❧ ❧ ❧

How to Read a Financial Report

Studying the financial statements of a company is perhaps the best way to determine its value as an investment. To obtain a copy of a company's annual report, simply write and ask for it. Once you invest in a business firm you will receive its financial statements and the annual report each year. A study of these statements will show you what the company is doing with your money and what you can expect in the way of earnings and growth.

The annual report shows the company's assets, liabilities, and earnings for the year. It may also provide information on product development, new merchandising techniques, the financial position of subsidiaries, changes in management, and other factors related to the overall performance of the company. While all of these factors are important in evaluating a company, we will concentrate on the financial statement for the present. Often there will be a separate statement of surplus. The basic parts of any financial statement are the *balance sheet* and the *income statement* (or *profit-and-loss statement*).

The Balance Sheet

The balance sheet sets forth a company's assets and liabilities at a given moment in time, usually as of the end of the fiscal year. The prior year's balance sheet is usually included in order to provide a meaningful contrast. Sometimes the annual report may include a 5- or 10-year financial summary which gives you an opportunity to check the company's progress over an extended period of time.

ASSETS in the balance sheet are divided into current, fixed, and other. Intangible assets such as goodwill, patents, trademarks, and copyrights are not usually listed.

Current Assets are so called because they can be converted into cash in a relatively short period of time. They include:

- *Cash and securities.*
- *Receivables*—amounts owed to the company by customers and others for goods sold and services rendered.
- *Inventories*—raw materials, work in process, supplies, and finished merchandise. To avoid overstating assets, inventories should be valued at cost or market price, whichever is lower. See page 135 for methods of valuing inventories.

- *Prepaid insurance* and other prepaid expenses.

Fixed Assets include property, machinery, and equipment, less depreciation reserves. Depreciation is a way of stating the wear and tear these assets have suffered to date and of spreading their costs over the years they are in use. Depletion is a similar provision to show the using up of assets consisting of natural resources. See page 136 for further discussion of depreciation and depletion reserves.

Other Assets outlined on the balance sheet include investments in nonconsolidated subsidiaries and miscellaneous investments.

LIABILITIES in the balance sheet include current liabilities, reserves, long-term debt, and stockholders' equity.

Current Liabilities represent amounts that are due and must be paid within a year. They include:

- *Accounts payable*—money owed for materials, supplies, and services used in operating the business.

- *Accrued liabilities*—amounts owed for such items as wages, salaries, commissions, pensions, interest.

- *Current maturities on long-term debts*—that portion of long-term debt coming due within the next year.

- *Federal income and other taxes.*

- *Interest payable*—amount due within the next year.

- *Dividends payable*—dividends on preferred and common stock declared but not yet paid. Once declared a dividend becomes an obligation.

Long-Term Debt refers to money borrowed but not payable in the next 12 months.

Stockholders' Equity shows the amount stockholders have invested in the business plus the earnings which have been accumulated and retained in the business. Types of stockholders' equity include:

- *Preferred stock*—preferred stockholders are entitled to be paid off ahead of common shareholders in liquidation and usually are entitled to a fixed dividend before dividends are paid on common stock.

- *Common stock*—the amount shown under this heading is usually based on an arbitrary amount at which the stock was put on the books.

- *Capital or paid-in surplus* (also called additional paid-in capital)—amount received for selling stock at more than par value.

- *Retained earnings*—accumulated earnings available for payment as dividends or reinvested in the business.

Now you have a brief explanation of the assets and liabilities outlined on the balance sheet in a company's financial statement. To fully understand how a company arrives at its statement of assets and liabilities you will also need to know where the company stands in regard to inventory valuation, depreciation and depletion allowances, and capital structure.

Inventory valuation is the method used to set a value of inventories. Of the various methods the first-in-first-out is the most common. It is based on the theory that the oldest items are used or sold before those recently purchased or produced. Companies using this method typically will have resulting higher profits during periods of rising prices.

Some companies have adopted the last-in-first-out method of valuing inventories. The purpose of this method is to match current costs against current prices. Sales costs are figured on the basis of inventory "last-in." First-in inventory is considered unsold. When prices are rising LIFO results in applying a higher unit cost to items sold and a lower unit cost to unsold inventory. This works in reverse when prices are falling.

Regardless of the method used to value inventories, keep in mind when you are evaluating a company that a large inventory or large increase from one year to the next can be risky. A sharp drop in prices could bring sizable losses. Large inventories can also mean that the company's sales policy is not as aggressive as is desirable—or that buying is not skillful.

Depreciation and depletion may appear as an expense on the income statement, and reserves for these expenses appear as a deduction from fixed assets on the balance sheet. Normally the fixed assets have a limited life and tend to decline in value for one of three reasons. They wear out or "depreciate." They are used up or "depleted" as happens in natural resource enterprises—lumber, oil, mining companies. They are outdated before wearing out or become "obsolete." Such was the case when propeller planes owned by the airlines had to be replaced by jets.

The *capital structure* of a company refers to the amount and sources of its capitalization—long-term debt, preferred stock, common stock, and retained earnings. Business enterprises can raise funds by means of stock, common and preferred, with various classes and restrictions. Money can be borrowed by the use of bonds and debentures, secured by specific assets, or by the general credit of the company. The combinations of these means are as varied as the companies themselves. Companies selling common stock only have what is called "simple" or "one-stock capitalization."

The investor's interest in a company varies. The holder of bonds or debentures is in fact a creditor of the company and as such has a first claim on assets. Preferred stockholders stand between creditors and common shareholders. Preferred stockholders normally are preferred over common shareholders in both the payment of dividends and in distribution of assets in liquidation. However, the preference in dividends is usually limited in amount. Preferred stockholders do not stand to gain as much from the company's growth. Common stockholders assume the greatest risk. They lose more in bad times and gain more in good times than other types of investors.

Statement of Income

The income statement summarizes all of the transactions over a given period which increase or decrease the value of the stockholders' share of the company. The income statement, in other words, shows the company's performance during the accounting period. It includes the following items:

Sales or *gross income* from operations is the first item on the income statement. It represents the total amount received from customers. When you are considering a company as an investment, look for a year-to-year increase in sales and a resulting increase in profits. Compare sales figures with other companies in the same industry.

137

Costs and expenses appear next on the income statement. These costs vary with the type of business. They are usually itemized as follows:

- *Cost of goods sold*—money paid out for wages, salaries, raw materials, supplies, and certain types of taxes.
- *Selling, administrative and other expenses*—money used for salesmen's commissions, advertising, officers' salaries, and general costs.
- *Depreciation and depletion*—allowances for the reduction in the service life of tools and buildings and the using up of natural resources.

Operating profit is the amount left from gross sales after deducting total operating costs and expenses. As a percentage of sales the operating profit shows the pretax profit margin.

Interest charges are next subtracted. This represents the amount required to pay interest due on borrowed funds.

Earnings before income taxes then result. These are the operating profits after interest charges.

Provision for federal and state taxes on income is just what it says—Uncle Sam's partnership interest in the business and that of the particular state.

Net income for the year is the profit after all expenses and deductions including taxes. This net profit is added to surplus.

Dividends on preferred stock may be listed on the income statement. The size of net income in relation to annual dividend requirements is particularly important in judging the investment quality of preferred stock. The question is, "how much could earnings shrink without endangering the payment of preferred dividends?"

Balance of net income available for common stock is the amount of net profit remaining after preferred dividends are deducted. This figure is normally used to figure common-stock earnings reduced to a per-share basis. To calculate per-share earnings on common stock, divide the balance of net income by the number of outstanding common shares.

Statement of Earned Surplus

The statement of earned surplus shows what part of the company's earnings have been retained and reinvested in the business. While earned surplus "belongs" to stockholders, the directors have decided it is better to reinvest this amount in the business. Normally retained earnings are not held in cash, but become part of other assets. They may be used to build up inventories, to repay indebtedness, or to expand plant and equipment. Reinvested earnings should eventually lead to increased earning ability.

The Accountant's Opinion

As a part of the financial statements you will find the accountant's report. It expresses the opinion of an independent expert skilled in accounting. This opinion normally states that the financial statements were prepared according to generally accepted accounting principles consistently applied, and that the statement fairly presents the financial position of the company at year-end and the results of operations during the period covered.

Evaluating a Company

You can evaluate a business as an investment value by applying certain objective tests to the financial statement. Investment analysts have established standards of acceptable performance based on relationships within the income statement and balance sheet and between the two. The following tests, applied to the financial statement of companies you are considering as investments, may help you decide which securities to buy.

The current or working capital ratio is the relationship of current assets to current liabilities. It is used primarily for industrial companies, and is an indication of the company's credit position. A two-to-one ratio—that is, current assets at twice the amount of current liabilities—is standard. A ratio of more than four or five to one is excessive. It may be caused by an insufficient volume of business to produce an adequate level of earnings.

The liquidity ratio, also known as quick net, is the relationship of cash and marketable securities to total current liabilities. This shows the company's ability to meet current obligations.

The sales-to-fixed assets ratio indicates whether or not funds used to expand productive facilities are being spent wisely. To figure the sales-to-fixed assets ratio, divide the annual sales by the value of fixed assets before depreciation and amortization. Normally a sizable expansion in facilities leads to greater sales volume. Such money put into expansion should bring in an appropriate return. However, the ratio of sales to fixed assets may suffer during the time it takes for demand to catch up to increased capacity. The ratio may be lower in a "heavy" industry—steel as compared to drugs. This is because plant investment is necessarily greater in heavy industries.

The inventory-turnover ratio dividing inventory into cost of sales shows how effectively moneys are used; showing whether the company has excessive inventory.

141

The net-income-to-net-worth ratio shows how much the company is earning on the stockholders' investment. To find this ratio, divide net income after taxes by the total of preferred stock, common stock, and surplus accounts. High ratios are most favorable. Surveys of all U.S. manufacturing corporations indicate that a return of over 10 percent is better than average. If you wish to compare the rates of return on stockholders' equity in different companies, check the *Quarterly Financial Report for Manufacturing Corporations* which is available from the U.S. Government Printing Office and the "Review of Corporate Profits in (year)" which appears in the April issue of *The Monthly Economic Letter* published by the First National City Bank of New York, 399 Park Avenue, New York, New York 10022.

Interest coverage is the relationship of interest charges to earnings. This shows how well the bondholders' interest is protected by earnings. To determine the ratio of earnings to interest charges, divide the net earnings or income before taxes (adding back interest charges) by the annual interest requirements. Interest coverage is figured before taxes because it is a claim prior to taxes.

Earnings per share on preferred stock show how well preferred dividends are protected by earnings.

The ratio is computed by dividing the net income by the number of shares of preferred stock.

Earnings per share on common stock show the dollar profit on each share of common stock outstanding.

Dividends per share of common stock simply show how much the company pays out as dividends on common stock. The board of directors usually sets up the company policy on dividends. Holders of common stock have no assurance of a fixed return. Dividends depend on earnings, the availability of funds, and the dividend policy. The dividend payout is the percentage of earnings on the common stock actually paid in dividends. Industrial companies pay out an average of about 55 percent of earnings in common-stock dividends. Because of their earnings stability, utility companies may pay 70 percent of earnings or more in dividends. Growth companies may pay considerably less due to the need of capital for expansion.

Book value per share of common stock is determined by adding the stated or par value of common stock to the capital surplus and retained earnings (deducting preferred stock at par), then dividing by the number of common shares. You can also figure the book value per common-stock share by deducting all liabilities and preferred stock from total assets. Then divide the remainder by the number of common shares. This gives you the book value, or the net assets per common share. In industrial companies where plant and equipment are the major assets, book value is not terribly important. The book value of common stocks is more significant in financial enterprises such as banks, insurance companies, and investment companies because their assets are largely current.

The price-earnings ratio is the market price of a stock divided by the earnings per share. Earnings per share are arrived at by dividing total earnings by the number of outstanding shares. If common stock is selling at $10 per share and earnings per share are $1, it is selling at 10 times earnings. This earnings figure has nothing to do with the dividends actually paid. Prices may run from 10 to 18 times earnings, but growth stocks may sell at over 40 times earnings. This is so because investors feel such stocks have greater potential and consequently are willing to pay more for them.

The dividend return, or yield, is found by dividing the annual dividend per share by the price of the stock. For instance, if a company pays a dividend of $4.20 per share on common stock which sells for $84, the dividend return is 5 percent—$4.20 divided by $84.

Information on securities is available from a variety of sources. The quarterly report published jointly by the Federal Trade Commission and the Securities and Exchange Commission publishes the average earnings and financial position of all manufacturing companies in the United States. It includes (1) the annual rate of profit on stockholders' equity at the end of each quarter—before and after federal income taxes (2) the ratio of current assets to current liabilities (3) the ratio of total cash and U.S. Government securities to total current liabilities, and (4) the ratio of total stockholders' equity to debt. While you may not want to go to the trouble of figuring and using all of the different financial tests or ratios, you may wish to apply the more meaningful ones to particular investments you are considering. Or, if you are not prepared to work out any of the financial relationships between figures found in the balance sheet and income statement of a company, you can obtain the judgment of market analysts through financial services. There is no reason ever to invest without first investigating.

A TYPICAL BALANCE SHEET

ASSETS, LIABILITIES, AND STOCKHOLDERS' EQUITY

ASSETS

Current Assets
Cash
U.S. Government securities
Accounts and notes receivable
Inventories
Prepaid insurance
    Total Current Assets

Other Assets
Surrender value of life insurance
Investments in subsidiaries
    Total Other Assets

Fixed Assets
Buildings, machinery, and equipment at cost
Less accumulated depreciation
Land
    Total Fixed Assets
        Total Assets

LIABILITIES AND STOCKHOLDERS' EQUITY

Current Liabilities
Accounts payable
Accrued liabilities
Federal income and other taxes
Current maturity of long-term debt
Dividends payable
    Total Current Liabilities

Long-Term Debt
5% sinking fund debentures, due July 31, 1976

Stockholders' Equity
5% cum. preferred stock ($100 par)
Common stock ($10 par)
Capital surplus or additional paid-in capital
Retained earnings
    Total Stockholders' Investment
    Total Liabilities and Stockholders' Equity

A TYPICAL STATEMENT OF INCOME

SALES

    Less:

    Costs and Expenses:

        Cost of goods sold

        Selling, general, and administrative expenses

        Depreciation and depletion

    Operating Profit

    Interest Charges

    Earnings Before Income Taxes

    Provision for Federal and State Taxes on Income

    Net Income for the Year

    Dividend on Preferred Stock

    Balance of Net Income Available for Common Stock

STATEMENT OF RETAINED EARNINGS

Balance at beginning of year

Add net income for the year

Less dividends paid on:

    Preferred stock

    Common stock

Balance at end of year

CHAPTER 9

✤ ✤ ✤

"The Professionals"
Who Can Help

No matter how knowledgeable you become in the investment world, you will not be ready to handle *all* aspects of managing your finances—any more than you are able to diagnose and treat your own illnesses. Much of your success in managing money depends on your ability to find and work with professionals in this field.

The Broker

Your broker is an agent, often a member of a stock exchange firm or an exchange member himself, who handles the public's orders to buy and sell securities or commodities. The broker's fee for buying or selling securities for a client is known as "commission." On the New York Stock Exchange, the average commission is about 1 percent of the market value of the stocks involved in the transaction and approximately .025 percent on bonds.

Most firms make no other charge for their services and advice. This includes custodial care for your securities—collecting dividends on stock and interest on bonds. If you have an open account with a broker, you generally will receive a monthly statement covering the status of your position.

MINIMUM NONMEMBER COMMISSION RATES ON STOCKS SELLING AT $1 PER SHARE AND ABOVE

On single transactions not exceeding 100 shares based upon the amount of money involved, the following rates apply:

ROUND LOTS

(A unit of trading, a combination of units of trading, or a combination of a unit or units of trading plus an odd lot, not exceeding 100 shares in all. The unit of trading in some issues on the New York Stock Exchange is 10 shares, while some issues on the American Exchange are traded in units of 50, 25, and 10 shares.)

Commission charges are $3 plus the total of 2 percent on the first $400, 1 percent on the next $2,000, ½ percent on the next $2,600, and 1/10 percent on all above $5,000.

To facilitate computation, charges can be stated as follows:

MONEY VALUE	COMMISSION
If less than $ 100.00	As mutually agreed
$ 100.00 to $ 399.99	2% plus $ 3.00
$ 400.00 to $2,399.99	1% plus $ 7.00
$2,400.00 to $4,999.99	½% plus $19.00
$5,000.00 and above	1/10% plus $39.00

ODD LOTS

(Less than a unit of trading)

Same rates as above, less $2.00, but in any case not less than $6.00 per transaction.

"THE PROFESSIONALS" ⚜ ⚜ ⚜

MINIMUM COMMISSIONS

(Notwithstanding above, each transaction is subject to the following):

When the amount involved in a transaction is less than $100, the minimum commission shall be as mutually agreed. When the amount involved in a transaction is $100 or more, the minimum commission charge shall not exceed $1.50 per share or $75 per single transaction, but in any event shall not be less than $6.00 per single transaction.

To determine the commission charge to be made on a transaction involving multiples of 100 shares, *e.g.*, 200, 300, 400, etc. shares, multiply the applicable 100 share commission by 2, 3, 4, etc., respectively, as the case may be.

If the broker is going to be an advisor, he should know your investment goals and financial circumstances so you and he can work together in the right direction. If he is merely a broker and takes your orders, the fact that it is a recommended firm will give you assurance that your orders will receive expert attention.* The firm should be recommended by your bank, your lawyer, your accountant, or any other knowledgeable, reliable, experienced person.

Opening an account with a reputable securities firm is much like opening a department-store charge account. Different firms specialize in various types of accounts. Some cater more to small accounts; others to institutional accounts, growth-type ac-

---

*Don't hesitate to ask for the firm's financial statement. If you can't read it, show it to your banker. Satisfy yourself on the firm's net capital.

CONFIRMATIONS—A written confirmation of every transaction is mailed to you. This gives all pertinent information concerning the transaction, from the name of the security to the net cost or credit after all fees and taxes. When you buy, the total cost will be charged to your account on the settlement day shown on the confirmation. The money to cover your purchase must be in your account by that time at the latest. When you sell securities the net proceeds will be credited to your account as of the settlement date and the securities you sold should be in the broker's hands by that time.

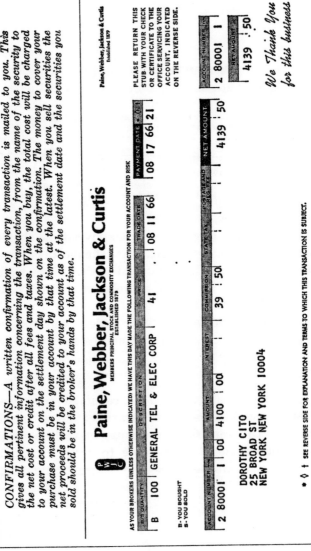

Paine, Webber, Jackson & Curtis

MEMBERS PRINCIPAL STOCK AND COMMODITY EXCHANGES
ESTABLISHED 1879

AS YOUR BROKERS (UNLESS OTHERWISE INDICATED) WE HAVE THIS DAY MADE THE FOLLOWING TRANSACTION FOR YOUR ACCOUNT AND RISK

B/S	QUANTITY	DESCRIPTION	PRICE	TRADE DATE	PAYMENT DATE
B	100	GENERAL TEL & ELEC CORP	41	08 11 66	08 17 66 21

ACCOUNT NUMBER		AMOUNT	INTEREST	COMMISSION	STATE TAX	POSTAGE AND REG. FEE	NET AMOUNT
2 8000 1 1	00	4100 00		39 50			4139 50

B - YOU BOUGHT
S - YOU SOLD

DOROTHY CITO
25 BROAD ST
NEW YORK NEW YORK 10004

* ◊ † SEE REVERSE SIDE FOR EXPLANATION AND TERMS TO WHICH THIS TRANSACTION IS SUBJECT.

Paine, Webber, Jackson & Curtis
Established 1879

PLEASE RETURN THIS STUB WITH YOUR CHECK OR CERTIFICATE TO THE OFFICE SERVICING YOUR ACCOUNT, INDICATED ON THE REVERSE SIDE.

ACCOUNT NUMBER
2 8000 1 1

NET AMOUNT
4139 50

We Thank You for this business

counts, or income-type accounts. Some take care of all types of accounts. Much depends upon the broker, also called the customer's man or the registered representative, in the particular firm. In my opinion, it is essential for this individual to be *trustworthy, knowledgeable,* and *capable of identifying with your circumstances yet remaining objective.*

The frequency with which you hear from your broker will depend upon the type of account you have. You should always feel free to call your broker. However, if he is a busy person, which most capable people are, you should not expect him to "chase" you. Think of him in terms of your doctor or your lawyer, who are as close as the telephone when you need their services!

If you are strictly investing, your broker may not be calling you at all. Rather he may wait to hear from you if you have questions, problems, or additional funds to invest—or if you want to reorient your account. For instance, suppose you are earning a handsome salary and your investment portfolio stresses appreciation, almost ignoring income. The time may come when you are ready to retire or are working less actively, thereby decreasing your income from employment. Then it would be desirable for you to increase income from your in-

MONTHLY STATEMENT—Your broker will send you each month a complete statement of your account with him if there has been any change from the previous month. This statement shows the securities you bought or sold during the month, a list of all of your securities in his possession, plus a record of your credit or debit balance. You should keep this statement, for it is a record of your transactions and your profits and losses. This information will be helpful to you when it comes time to file your income tax.

IN ACCOUNT WITH

PAINE, WEBBER, JACKSON & CURTIS

MEMBERS PRINCIPAL STOCK AND COMMODITY EXCHANGES
ESTABLISHED 1879

PLEASE MENTION YOUR FULL ACCOUNT NUMBER ON ALL CHECKS AND COMMUNICATIONS. REPORT ANY DIFFERENCES IMMEDIATELY TO THE OFFICE SERVICING YOUR ACCOUNT INDICATED ON REVERSE SIDE.

ACCOUNT NUMBER

2 80001

TYPE OF ACCOUNT

1—2—3—4—5—6—7—8—9

CASH
GENERAL
SUBSCRIPTION
SHORT
INCOME
NON-PURPOSE LOAN
NON-REG. COMDY.*
ON-REG. COMDY.*
CUSTODIAN

FOR PERIOD ENDING
MONTH 25 DAY YEAR 66
AUG

DOROTHY CITO
25 BROAD ST
NEW YORK NY 10004

DATE	BOUGHT RECEIVED OR LONG	SOLD DELIVERED OR SHORT	DESCRIPTION	PRICE	DEBIT	CREDIT	BALANCE DEBIT UNLESS MARKED CR	TYPE
			BAL FWD JULY 28 1966			4745 30		--
AUG 11	100		GENERAL TEL & ELEC CORP	41				--
AUG 12			CHECK		4139 50			--
AUG 15		25	ACF INDUSTRIES INC	49 1/8		4139 50		--
						1209 57		
	50		BORDEN CO					--
	100		GENERAL TEL & ELEC CORP					--
	25		DU PONT DE NEMOURS					--
	25		STANDARD OIL N J				5954 87CR	--
	100		F W WOOLWORTH					--

NOTICE – PRESERVE THIS STATEMENT TO ASSIST IN PREPARING INCOME TAX RETURNS.

IF WE MAINTAIN A SPECIAL MISCELLANEOUS ACCOUNT FOR YOU UNDER FEDERAL RESERVE REGULATION T, SECTION 4 (f) (6), IT HAS BEEN CONSOLIDATED IN THE STATEMENT OF YOUR GENERAL ACCOUNT. THE PERMANENT RECORD OF THE SPECIAL MISCELLANEOUS ACCOUNT IS AVAILABLE FOR YOUR INSPECTION UPON REQUEST. FUNDS OR SECURITIES DUE TO OR FROM THIS ACCOUNT ARE (A) NOT CREATED NOR MAY BE USED IN THE OPERATION OF THIS FIRM'S BUSINESS; AND (B) ARE PAYABLE ON DEMAND. SUCH FUNDS, ALTHOUGH NOT SEGREGATED, ARE PROPERLY ACCOUNTED FOR ON OUR BOOKS OF RECORD.

A FINANCIAL STATEMENT OF THIS FIRM IS AVAILABLE FOR YOUR PERSONAL INSPECTION AT ITS OFFICES, OR A COPY WILL BE MAILED UPON YOUR WRITTEN REQUEST.

CA-21-4

vestments. You might talk this over with your broker and switch some of your holdings based on these changed circumstances.

Your broker has a record of your holdings if you have purchased them from him. If he is doing a conscientious job, you should be hearing from him when there is noteworthy news with reference to these holdings, or if he is service-minded, you may be kept informed even when there is no action required but merely because he wants to keep you up-to-date. May I inject a personal word here—namely, that the pleasure of working with someone who takes this personal interest is what makes you feel you are a person rather than an account number!

If you are a trader, you will be talking to your broker a great deal—hourly, daily, weekly fluctuations could mean much—hopefully for taking profits, maybe to limit losses, generally to keep close track of short-term price movements. A trader is a person who buys and sells hoping to make a profit. This is no kid's game. It requires limiting losses, i.e., admitting something is—for a reason or for no reason—not working. At times it requires taking profits and then seeing the price soar afterwards. My old saying is that he who buys at the low and sells at the high is doing it by accident. A true trader takes both profits and losses coldbloodedly!

The two basic orders which you would most likely give your broker are:

- *The market order*—to buy or sell a stated number of a specific security immediately at the most advantageous price obtainable when the order reaches the trading crowd. In other words, this is an order to buy or sell at the prevailing price at the time the order is executed.

- *The limited order or limited price order*—to buy or sell only at a specified price or better, when and if that price is obtainable. The order may *not* be executed at a less advantageous price than that stated.

Variations of these two orders may be advantageous under certain circumstances related to time of an order or the amount involved. The variations include:

- *An at-the-close order*—a market order to be executed as near as possible to the close of the day's trading.

- *An at-the-opening order*—a market o r d e r or limited price order to be executed when the market opens or not at all.

- *A day order*—a buy or sell order which, unless executed, expires at the end of the trading day on which it is entered.

- *A good-till-canceled, or open order*—just what it says, an order to buy or sell which is good until executed or until canceled.

- *A stop order*—an order to buy or sell at a specified price. It becomes effective only when the price of the stock reaches the price specified by the buyer or seller. The stop order is used to protect profits and limit losses.

Here's how the stop order limits losses. You buy 100 shares of stock at $25 per share. You want to limit losses to $500 so you give your broker a *stop order* to sell at $20 per share. If the stock does drop to that amount, your stop order becomes a market order. If the stock advances the stop order is not executed and your profits grow.

You can also use the stop order to protect profits when a stock advances to a certain amount. Suppose in the above order, the stock advances to $45 per share and you want to protect a profit of $1,000. You place a stop order to sell at $35 per share. If the stock drops back to $35, your stop order is executed as a market order and you have your profit of $1,000. If the stock continues to go up, you keep your shares and your profits increase.

Stop orders to buy are used to limit losses on short sales. See Glossary.

As you become a more sophisticated investor, you will need to understand other types of orders and procedures in buying and selling securities. For instance, you may buy securities either in odd lots or round lots.

An *odd lot* refers to any number of shares less than a round lot or trading unit. A round lot or trading unit is normally 100—but sometimes 10—shares. When you purchase shares in odd lots, your broker places your order through an odd-lot dealer. When the stock sells under $55, an odd-lot dealer usually executes your order 1/8th point (12½ cents) away from the price of the next round lot sale or the current bid or offer price. If the stock is $55 or above, the differential will be 1/4th point or 25 cents rather than 12½ cents.

Odd lot orders as small as one share can be executed. The methods of handling odd-lot orders are so perfected that you receive prompt, efficient service no matter how small your order may be.

In buying securities, you either pay cash or buy *on margin*. Cash purchases of securities are like paying cash for anything else. You pay the cost of the securities plus commissions in cash. Buying on margin is different—it involves a credit arrangement with your broker.

The amount of credit available to you is based on the initial margin requirement, which is determined by the Federal Reserve Board. (Initial refers to the margin rate at the time of your original purchase.)

When a margin rate of 70 percent is in effect this means simply that if you want to buy listed stock on credit, you have to put up 70 percent of the market value of the stock in cash.

If the rate were 50 percent, you would have to put up 50 percent cash.

For instance: Assuming a rate of 70 percent margin, you are able to buy $5,000 worth of listed securities for $3,500 in cash (or $11,670 in listed securities as collateral). The stock you buy is collateral for the credit your broker provides. Your broker puts up the balance—a service for which he charges, of course, because usually he uses his own credit in your behalf and in turn is charged for the loan he gets at the bank.

If the price of the stock you buy advances, you have nothing to worry about. If the price declines enough, you may have a problem.

Once you have purchased stock, your margin changes as the price changes.

Here's an example. You have bought 100 shares at $50 a share on a margin of 70 percent. Your equity is $3,500. The price rises to $55 a share and your equity increases to $4,000—the $5 a share increase multiplied by 100 shares. Your margin has increased to 72.7 percent although you still must pay your broker the $1,500 he provided, an amount also known as your net debit balance.

Margin can be calculated by this simple formula:

$$\text{Margin} = \frac{\text{Market Value of Securities Minus Amount Put Up by Broker}}{\text{Market Value of Securities}}$$

Thus, at $55 a share, your margin would work out this way.

$$\text{Margin} = \frac{\$5,500 - \$1,500}{\$5,500} = 72.7 \text{ percent}$$

If the price of the stock declines to $45, your equity drops to $3,000 ($4,500—$1,500) and your margin is 66.6 percent. Thus:

$$\text{Margin} = \frac{\$4,500 - \$1,500}{\$4,500} = 66.6 \text{ percent}$$

The Federal Reserve determines only the initial margin. The New York Stock Exchange, however, requires that you must maintain a minimum margin of 25 percent—that is, your equity must amount to no less than 25 percent of the market value of the stock.

As a matter of practice, however, most member firms of the Stock Exchange have their own minimum maintenance margin requirements, usually between 30 percent and 35 percent of the market value of a security.

Here's an easy way to figure out if you need additional margin on the basis of a 25 percent or a 33⅓ percent minimum maintenance margin:

On a 25 percent minimum maintenance basis (assuming a 70 percent initial Federal Reserve margin requirement), you would need additional margin if the price of your stock declined approximately 60 percent. On a 33⅓ percent minimum maintenance basis, you would need additional margin if your stock declined by 55 percent.

This can be expressed in still another way—a method, in fact, used in the back offices of many brokerage firms. A firm which requires 25 percent minimum will call for additional margin when the market value of the stock in the account falls to less than 1⅓ times the customer's net debit balance. For example, the customer has purchased $10,000 worth of securities on 70 percent margin. His net debit balance is $3,000; 1⅓ the net debit balance is $4,000. Therefore, when the market value of the customer's securities falls to $4,000—a decline of 60 percent—the broker will call for additional margin.

Applying this concept to a 33⅓ percent minimum margin requirement, the multiple applied to the net debit balance is 1½. Thus, $10,000 in securities purchased on 70 percent margin creates a net debit balance of $3,000; 1½ times the debit balance is $4,500. Therefore, when the customer's securities fall to $4,500—a decline of 55 percent—the broker will call for additional margin.

The Stock Exchange itself has another regulation governing margin accounts—no margin account, as a general rule, may be opened with a balance of less than $1,000. Several member firms have even higher requirements on margin accounts.

The *short sale* mystifies most beginning investors since it involves selling something you do not own. This is basically an area for the experienced investor. The short sale is a way of making a profit when the market or a specific stock *declines*. Here's how:

Suppose a particular stock is selling at $50 per share and you think it will go lower. You call your broker and instruct him to sell short 100 shares of the stock at $50. You put up $3,500, or 70 percent of the price of the shares since a short sale is subject to the current margin requirement. He executes your order by selling the stock (which you *do not own*) and then borrowing 100 shares of that stock to deliver to the buyer. At a later date, when you want to close the transaction, you give your broker an order to buy 100 shares of the stock and return it to the lender.

Suppose you are right and the stock drops to $45 per share. When you buy the 100 shares to cover the sale, you make a profit of $500 less commissions, taxes, etc.* If you made a mistake and the stock advanced, you would lose the difference between the price at which you bought and the price at which you sold—plus commissions and taxes. The stock exchanges and federal laws set forth special rules which apply to short selling.

The Investment Counselor

The previous section on the broker explained that he frequently counsels you in setting up an investment program and building a suitable portfolio. However, you may want to call on other profes-

---

*Less any dividends which are declared during the period you are "short," because the person lending the stock is entitled to the dividend.

sionals for advice and service related to specific aspects of managing your personal finances. One of these is the investment counselor.

The *investment counselor* is a professional whose job it is to provide investment advice and supervision. For a fee, he makes investment decisions for his clients and channels buy and sell orders through a brokerage firm. There are over 300 of these investment counseling services around the country. This professional serves primarily individual investors who invest large amounts—generally $100,000 or more—although there is a trend toward $50,000 accounts with a slightly higher fee. The counselor also serves institutional investors.

If you are in a position to use the services of an investment counselor, finding the right man—or firm—is all important. Shop around to see how different counselors evaluate your investment needs. Get across your personal objectives and find the counselor who can do the best job of helping you reach your goals—be it income, growth, safety, or a combination of these. One way to evaluate a counselor is to find out what advice he has given others at certain critical periods in the market.

You can obtain varying degrees of service from an investment counselor—ranging from mere advice to complete management of your portfolio. If your investable funds are not great enough to call upon the investment counselor, numerous other advisory services are available to you. They include Standard and Poor's Corporation and Moody's Investor's Service, along with several other types of investment advisory services. You will find a variety of services available—compilation of statistics related to investments, recommendations about specific securities, review of business conditions, answers to questions from investors and tailor-made services—all for a fee.

The Banker

Your *banker* is another professional whose services are frequently related to your investment plans and overall financial program. For the most part, your main business with your bank is connected with depositing or withdrawing money—by making a visit or, as many of us do, by mail. Yet your bank offers a variety of services for sophisticated and effective financial planning. The trust department in most banks offers:

- *Custodial arrangements.* This means the bank takes physical care of your securities, including collection of dividends on stock and interest on bonds. You may want this service if you are unable or do not care to give these matters the time and attention required. The usual charge for custodial service is a percentage of the portfolio value.

- *Investment management,* which means continuous supervision and analysis of a portfolio, making buy and sell recommendations, and considering tax status.

- *Trust administration,* which means that the bank, as trustee, manages your assets. The trust can be set up for administration during your lifetime or after death. Such an arrangement may offer tax advantages and can protect beneficiaries. It may also keep the assets in trust from going through probate.

- *Estate administration,* which includes overseeing probate, taking an inventory of assets, checking life-insurance coverage, settling debts, paying taxes and bequests, etc. Banks are frequently named sole or coexecutor for an estate because they are financially informed and almost certain to outlive the individuals involved.

If you are not already dealing with a bank that offers the personal attention you want, start shopping. Banks differ in many ways. Nowadays most banks make a real effort to serve women effectively. In fact, many large banks have women's departments. In choosing a bank consider the services available and the fees you pay for various services.

To a woman, says Jessamine Durante, head of the women's division of Chicago's Harris Trust & Savings Bank, security is an important objective in her life. In building this secure framework, she desires an ordered financial arrangement for herself and those she cares for most—her family. An underlying problem which she faces is lack of knowledge concerning the management of her income to provide this security. The problem is intensified when she seeks long-term security.

For help in both these areas, a woman today need only turn to her bank. Here she will find those who *know* how to help her attain her objectives. They are anxious to give assistance. Anxious, in many cases, to do the work for her.

The service function used most by woman is, of course, the checking account. Through this service, she can deposit all funds received, pay bills with ease and convenience, and be provided with receipts of all deposits and payments. Keeping additional records is all but eliminated with the proper use of her checking account. And all these transactions can be handled easily by mail.

A systemized savings plan is the cornerstone for all financial security. She can make regular monthly payments into her savings account by having the money automatically transferred from her checking account on a certain date each month. For holding larger amounts of money (beyond what would be needed in the case of an emergency), she can purchase savings certificates and certificates of deposit which bear higher interest rates. These will be automatically renewed at maturity dates, if such is her wish.

Emergencies, by definition, are happenings which are unexpected, and they invariably occur when they are least expected. The bank can meet these emergencies for today's woman by lending her money quickly and economically. Other large outlays of cash which cannot, and probably should not, be taken care of from savings, can be arranged for with a bank loan. Reasons for such cash requirements might include purchase of real estate, an automobile, or home improvements. A convenient, but realistic, repayment program will erase the loan and leave her savings account intact.

For the woman who travels extensively, either for business or pleasure, the bank takes over the role of "next door neighbor." A safe deposit box can be arranged for which will accommodate all her important documents and valuable possessions. Stock certificates, bonds, mortgage agreements, heirlooms, insurance policies, household inventories, income-tax records, and valuable jewelry receive the protection and privacy they deserve.

Corporations in which she holds stock can be instructed to send dividend payments directly to her bank where they will immediately be deposited into her checking or savings account, whichever she chooses. No chance of their getting lost in the deluge of mail which will arrive in her absence.

If her travels take her abroad, the bank takes over where her travel agent leaves off. Traveler's checks are available, of course, but also she can obtain at the bank small packs of foreign currencies to get her through foreign airports, providing some necessary money for tipping, and perhaps a taxi ride to the hotel where she can conveniently convert to local currency. In addition, the bank will be happy to send funds ahead to her travel destination, issue letters of credit, and write letters of introduction to foreign banks.

Now that banks are in the credit-card business, women can take advantage of just one more valuable service. As banks iron out the problems of a compatible national-bank-card system, her charge card will be honored at business establishments all over the country. Establishing credit will be greatly simplified for her at home and out of town if she carries her bank charge card. It represents the confidence of a major bank in her ability to pay.

In addition to providing for current expenses out of current income, a woman for her own peace of mind must establish a plan to amass enough capital to support her at a time when she is no longer working. If she is married, this can be a joint effort, but many working women will be supporting themselves when the paychecks no longer arrive. Today's woman can turn to her bank for investment counseling on a personal basis. Depending on her own situation, many roads to financial security are available. Systematic saving is, of course, the first step. Logically, investment of these funds follows. Some banks are equipped to handle all the details of the purchase and sale of government bonds (in small and large amounts) and tax-exempt state and municipal bonds. Advice as to investments in these low-risk securities and in corporate stocks is hers for the asking from experts in this field. In fact, the bank will go one step further. Its trust department will assume control of her investment account for her—take physical possession of the securities, collect and deposit the dividend payments, exercise rights and warrants, and periodically review the portfolio with suggestions to buy or sell, depending on her long-term goals. Constant attention by experts is what her investments deserve and get.

Setting up a trust fund to provide for herself and her family, even after her death, might be a wise move. A bank is well-equipped in this field to act as trustee on her behalf—to assume the duties of managing her property prudently, producing the highest income consistent with safety, and distributing the income according to her instructions. She will also want to name the bank as executor under her will to see that her estate is handled with proper technical skill, experience, impartiality, and financial responsibility.

For the woman who owns and/or manages her own business, a good bank is her right arm in all financial matters. Her banker can even take an active part in finding an office or plant location, suggesting competent executive personnel, or locating a buyer if she is interested in selling her business. If her company is an international marketer or would like to be, a host of services are available from skilled international bankers. To reward the service and contribution of good employees, the bank might assist her in establishing pension and profit-sharing plans for their benefit.

Having cash available at the proper time, without allowing it to sit idle for long periods, is a problem common to all businesses. Optimum use of bank services will eliminate this problem for the woman manager. The bank can provide financial counseling on a continuing basis. If available funds will be needed in the near future, the bank might suggest temporary investment in short-term securities for the best return, and handle all the details of the transaction. In order for her to make long-term investments and to meet short-term commitments, bank loans can be conveniently arranged. If she is in a retail field, the bank is equipped to handle her company's credit function through the use of the charge-card plan.

The cost of these services is small; many of them are completely free. Establishment with a good bank can be a woman's best investment in her future.

The Accountant

Accountants normally are employed by large firms and their services for the most part are limited to the business world rather than the individual. It is the accountant who prepares the financial statements that tell you so much of what you should know before buying the securities of a company.

If you use the accountant's services on an individual basis, it will most likely be in connection with income-tax returns—this is one of his specialties. Like the other professionals who serve you, the accountant relies on you to provide the pertinent information—the necessary facts and figures—to complete your tax return. Of course, he will collect much of this data from your records—with an eye for what he needs to know. His services may be of special help when your investments become so successful as to contribute a major share of your income each year. The accountant is an expert in handling tax problems and securing tax benefits for you where possible.

TAX CONSIDERATIONS

Among the tax considerations you may want to discuss with your accountant are the following:

A. Capital Gains:

1. Profit from sales of securities receive special treatment if held for more than six months. The gains from such sales are termed long-term capital gains and are taxed at 50 percent of the regular tax rates with a maximum tax of 25 percent.

2. Gains on disposition of securities held for six months or less are taxed at regular tax rates.

B. Offsetting Losses and Gains:

1. Capital losses may be used to offset capital gains. If the losses on sales of securities exceed the gains, the excess up to $1,000 per year may be applied against ordinary income.

2. The unused capital loss may be carried over as a "capital-loss carryover" and treated as a capital loss incurred in future years. The amount which can be used in any one future year is again limited to the amount of capital gains in that year plus $1,000.

C. Tax Benefits Through Gifts of Income-Producing Stock:

1. An individual can give any one donee $3,000 each year without creating any gift tax liability; a married couple can give $6,000.

2. Once in a lifetime, each individual can give an additional $30,000 in total with no gift tax liability.

3. If the donee is a dependent child, parent or other relative, the family's total income tax will be reduced, as the income from the property given will thereafter be taxable to the dependent, in a lower tax bracket than the donor's.

4. The property given away may be eliminated from the donor's taxable estate, thereby producing an additional saving in the form of federal and state estate and inheritance taxes. Since gift tax rates begin at 2¼ percent, it may even be advisable to expand the program of gifts to a point where gift tax is incurred, as the other tax savings may exceed the modest gift tax liability.

The Attorney

Whether your fortune is large or small, an *attorney* will be one of your most important counselors in all areas. His services may be related primarily to tax problems, trusts, wills, and estate planning. He may want to work with your accountant on your tax and estate matters. He may find ways to save tax dollars for you by taking care of the routine aspects of preparing and filing tax returns—availing you of all that is coming to you. He will consider with you the advisability of setting up trusts which provide for managing your property for your beneficiaries during your lifetime or after your death. These trust arrangements may have major tax benefits for you.

This takes us back to the point that no intelligent person with any property of consequence should be without a will and certainly no intelligent person should attempt to write his own will. The laws governing wills and probate are extremely complicated and require the skills of an attorney. The only way to be sure that your assets are distributed according to your wishes is to work with a competent lawyer in drawing up a will. I was once party to a case in which a husband and wife died in an automobile accident—leaving no will. It was established that one of the two survived the other by a matter of minutes—and this person's relatives were the *sole* heirs. How unfortunate—and unnecessary! In this case, it was particularly sad since the heirs were already wealthy while the other family was not.

Your lawyer can help you draw a will for distribution of your assets according to *your* wishes— and avoid difficulties. If you are married, he can help you decide whether it is desirable for you and your husband to draw separate wills or a mutual will.

Wills and Estate Planning

A will is a real necessity unless you are completely indifferent to how your estate is divided up and how much of your assets are eaten up by taxes and expenses. The chief advantages of a well-drawn will include the following:

- You can avoid the expense of a surety bond. This alone will generally more than cover the cost of having an attorney draw your will.

- Your assets are distributed according to your desires.

- You can arrange for great savings on estate and inheritance taxes.

- You can name an executor of your choosing to manage the estate and trustees to manage property after the estate is closed, if necessary.

- You can name a guardian for minor children.

In the absence of a will, property is distributed according to state law which varies from state to state. In some states, when a man dies without a will—where there is a surviving spouse *and* descendants—the spouse receives only one-third of the estate and descendants receive the remaining two-thirds. If there are no descendants the entire estate *may* go to the surviving spouse—but in some states, part of the estate is distributed to the parents or brothers and sisters of the deceased. Such a scheme of distribution of assets is, in effect, a will drawn up for everyone by the state legislature and may not accomplish what you want and need.

Your attorney can help you draw a will ensuring that your affairs will be settled according to your wishes. Discuss the matter with your attorney openly and frankly. Give him a clear picture of your circumstances and tell him all of your desires, no matter how insignificant they may seem. As with other important personal matters so it is with a will —your attorney and other professionals who serve you should collaborate in order to achieve your goals. Your attorney may want to confer with your banker, your insurance man, your accountant, and your broker, or with any one of them. Matters for them to jointly consider include:

- Your estate in the light of estate and inheritance taxes.
- How property such as stock and real estate is held— whether in your name alone or jointly with your spouse.
- Status of your insurance policies—who are the beneficiaries? Are benefits to be paid into a trust or outright in a lump sum or installment?

If you have an estate of fairly substantial size, trusts of various types should be explored. They frequently offer tax advantages and protection for beneficiaries. A trust may be set up to commence during one's lifetime and continue after death—or to commence at death. Also, in the case of larger estates, it is often advantageous from a tax standpoint to set up a systematic program of gift-giving during your lifetime. Such a program, one of trusts, life insurance, lifetime gifts, and a will, all carefully coordinated, constitute an estate plan by which a good attorney can save large sums of money for your family and provide for the maximum well-being of everyone near and dear to you.

Once you have drawn your will and made other provisions, keep in mind that both your circumstances and the laws pertaining to taxes and inheritance change from time to time. It is important to review your situation every few years—or sooner if changes occur. Wills and estate planning provide a means for you to provide for and protect your family even after your death. Such careful planning brings peace of mind and a sense of security. Is it not a great feeling to know that—in life and in death—order, intelligence, and able management of your affairs prevail? Our great fortunes could not have been perpetuated without proper structure and planning. Think like a millionaire, because it brings results!

Among the numerous other things on which your attorney can give you valuable advice are the advantages and disadvantages of joint ownership of property if you are married. If you are widowed, he can aid you in matters pertaining to your husband's estate and, based on your new circumstances, help you plan your future. If you own real estate, if you have a business of your own, or if you are party to any contractual arrangements, your lawyer should advise you *and* formulate the proper protection for you—to avoid future complications.

One thing to remember *always* is to ask your lawyer *before* signing or deciding on matters of importance. Don't wait for an emergency to find a lawyer—any more than you would wait for an appendix attack to find a doctor. Have a legal checkup regularly! Choose an attorney as you would any of your professionals—preferably through your bank, a reliable business or personal associate, or through the local bar association.

It is desirable for your "professionals" to work together as a team in order to serve you most effectively. You in turn must be completely honest and cooperative with them. Just one piece of important information withheld can dramatically alter your case.

You gain a sense of security when you are in the hands of competent professionals—it spells safety, comfort, tranquility. It contributes to the peace of mind which we constantly seek in all endeavors. And proper management of ourselves is the only way we can achieve it—financially, physically, or emotionally.

CHAPTER 10

✤ ✤ ✤

Epilogue

One of my friends was terribly apologetic recently because it was inconvenient for him to drop me off in front of my building. Comfortingly I turned to him and said, "Now that we girls have grabbed the fruits of emancipation and are holding them so tightly, I feel ever so occasionally we can take the short end and walk across the street by ourselves!" He graciously conceded the point.

Along a more serious vein, I do want to end this book by emphasizing the philosophy which we try to instill in our children, into all friendship, in business and human relationships of every type—namely, that with *privilege comes responsibility!*

How do I apply this to the financial? Easy—if we girls want to relish the fact that we are a major segment of the "financial population" in this twentieth century, we must not shirk the responsibilities that ensue. We want to have our cake and eat it. Many times we have that and more—if we have a man who loves, cherishes, protects, spoils us as only the American male knows how.

I do not want to make my main case the financial crisis of widowhood, which is the real "threat" to the married woman. Nor is it my objective to point up "going it alone," which may be a real "threat" to the woman who never marries or who is divorced and as a result has to do her own financial planning. My main objective is to point up the challenge of being independent, knowledgeable, and deserving one's privileges as a woman. When married, what a delicious community of interest to plan together, to spend and save together. If unmarried, what great joy and satisfaction comes with the capacity to earn, to save, to spend, and to shape one's own life.

This book should serve only as an eye-opener and reference source. If you are inspired to the point that you want to know more, the answer is to take courses at a university or college. The first ones may not sound too impressive, but accomplishments pile up with time. When I first started to go to night school at Northwestern University, the advice I received was most discouraging. In fact, almost all I heard was that it would take me forever to cover the courses I needed and wanted. It did—but to use a worn-out expression, I must say that "getting there was half the fun." The inspiration from instructors who lived and breathed economics was unforgettable. This made the battle worthwhile—walking east on Chicago Avenue to the "Tower of Knowledge" on windy nights in this cold city. The excitement of life is endless; from living, learning, gaining direction and momentum as we go along. If I sound contagious, I mean to be!

✤ ✤ ✤

The Language of Investing

The professional words and phrases used in the investment world, often vivid and colorful, will be found in the following glossary, for which the author is indebted to the New York Stock Exchange.

Some words and expressions have filtered down from the days when brokers traded securities in the open air, under the shade of a buttonwood tree. Others have come into the language of Wall Street during the computer age. Additional information concerning any word or phrase descriptive of a market operation can be obtained without obligation by asking any member firm of the New York Stock Exchange or by calling or writing the exchange itself.

Whenever the opportunity affords, the reader is urged to visit the great trading floor of the New York Stock Exchange. A visitors' gallery is available, and well-informed receptionists will tell you everything that is happening and answer any questions about a dynamic "people's capitalism" at work.

ACCRUED INTEREST: Interest accrued on a bond since the last interest payment was made. The buyer of the bond pays the market price plus accrued interest. Exceptions include bonds which are in default and income bonds. (See: *Flat, Income Bond*)

ALL-OR-NONE ORDER: A market or limited-price order which is to be executed in its entirety or not at all, but, unlike a fill-or-kill order, is not to be treated as canceled if not executed as soon as it is represented in the trading crowd. Bids or offers on behalf of all-or-none orders may not be made in stocks, but may be made in bonds when the number of bonds is 50 or more. (See: *Trading Crowd*)

185

ALTERNATING ORDER—EITHER/OR ORDER: An order to do either of two alternatives—such as, either sell (buy) a particular stock at a limit price or sell (buy) on stop. If the order is for one unit of trading when one part of the order is executed on the happening of one alternative, the order on the other alternative is treated as canceled. If the order is for an amount larger than one unit of trading, the number of units executed determines the amount of the alternative order to be treated as canceled.

AMORTIZATION: A generic term. Includes various specific practices such as depreciation, depletion, write-off of intangibles, prepaid expenses, and deferred charges.

ANNUAL REPORT: The formal financial statement issued yearly by a corporation to its shareowners. The annual report shows assets, liabilities, earnings—how the company stood at the close of the business year and how it fared profit-wise during the year.

ARBITRAGE: A technique employed to take advantage of differences in price. If, for example, XYZ stock can be bought in New York for $10 a share and sold in London at $10.50, an arbitrageur may simultaneously purchase XYZ stock here and sell the same amount in London, making a profit of 50 cents a share, less expenses. Arbitrage may also involve the purchase of rights to subscribe to a security, or the purchase of a convertible security—and the sale at or about the same time of the security obtainable through exercise of the rights or of the security obtainable through conversion. (See: *Convertible, Rights*)

ASSETS: Everything a corporation owns or due to it: Cash, investments, money due it, materials and inventories, which are called current assets; buildings and machinery, which are known as fixed assets; and patents and good will, called intangible assets. (See: *Liabilities*)

AT-THE-CLOSE ORDER: A market order which is to be executed at or as near to the close of a day's trading as practicable.

AT-THE-OPENING OR AT-THE-OPENING-ONLY ORDER: A market or limited price order which is to be executed at the opening of trading or not at all, and any such order or portion thereof not so executed is treated as canceled.

186

THE LANGUAGE OF INVESTING   ⚜ ⚜ ⚜

AVERAGES: Various ways of measuring the trend of securities prices, the most popular of which is the Dow-Jones average of 30 industrial stocks listed on the New York Stock Exchange. The term average has led to considerable confusion. A simple average for, say, 50 leading stocks would be obtained by totaling the prices of all and dividing by 50. But suppose one of the stocks in the average is split. The price of each share of that stock is then automatically reduced because more shares are outstanding. Thus the average would decline even if all other issues in the average were unchanged. That average thus becomes inaccurate as an indicator of the market's trend.

Various formulas—some very elaborate—have been devised to compensate for stock splits and stock dividends and thus give continuity to the average. Averages and individual stock prices belong in separate compartments.

In the case of the Dow-Jones industrial average, the prices of the 30 stocks are totaled and then divided by a divisor which is intended to compensate for past stock splits and dividends and which is changed from time to time. As a result point changes in the average have only the vaguest relationship to dollar price changes in stocks included in the average. In November, 1965, the divisor was 2.245, so that a one-point change in the industrial average at that time was actually the equivalent of 7 cents.

The New York Stock Exchange reports its own daily indices, based on dollars-and-cents averages of all stocks traded and of special groups of stocks. (See: *Point, Split*)

AVERAGING: (See: *Dollar-Cost Averaging*)

BALANCE SHEET: A condensed statement showing the nature and amount of a company's assets, liabilities, and capital on a given date. In dollar amounts the balance sheet shows what the company owned, what it owed, and the ownership interest in the company of its stockholders. (See: *Assets, Earnings Report*)

BEAR: Someone who believes the market will decline. (See: *Bull*)

BEAR MARKET: A declining market. (See: *Bull Market*)
BEARER BOND: A bond which does not have the owner's name registered on the books of the issuing company and which is payable to the holder. (See: *Coupon Bond, Registered Bond*)

187

BID AND ASKED: Often referred to as a quotation or quote. The bid is the highest price anyone has declared that he wants to pay for a security at a given time, the asked is the lowest price anyone will take at the same time. (See: *Quotation*)

BIG BOARD: A popular term for the New York Stock Exchange.

BLUE CHIP: Common stock in a company known nationally for the quality and wide acceptance of its products or services, and for its ability to make money and pay dividends. Usually such stocks are relatively high priced and offer relatively low yields.

BLUE-SKY LAWS: A popular name for laws various states have enacted to protect the public against securities frauds. The term is believed to have originated when a judge ruled that a particular stock had about the same value as a patch of blue sky.

BOARD ROOM: A room for customers in a broker's office where opening, high, low, and last prices of leading stocks are posted on a board throughout the market day.

BOILER ROOM: High-pressure peddling over the telephone of stocks of dubious value. A typical boiler room is simply a room lined with desks or cubicles, each with a salesman and telephone. The salesmen call what is known in the trade as sucker lists.

BOND: Basically an IOU or promissory note of a corporation, usually issued in multiples of $1,000, although $100 and $50 denominations are not uncommon. A bond is evidence of a debt on which the issuing company usually promises to pay the bondholders a specified amount of interest for a specified length of time, and to repay the loan on the expiration date. In every case a bond represents debt—its holder is a creditor of the corporation and not a part owner as is the shareholder. (See: *Collateral Trust Bond, Convertible, General Mortgage Bond, Income Bond*)

BOOK: A notebook the specialist in a stock uses to keep a record of the buy and sell orders at specified prices, in strict sequence of receipt, which are left with him by other brokers. (See: *Specialist*)

BOOK VALUE: An accounting term. Book value of a stock is determined from a company's records, by adding all assets (generally excluding such intangibles as good will), then deducting all debts and other liabilities, plus the liquidation price of any preferred issues. The sum arrived at is divided by the number of common shares outstanding and the result is book value per common share. Book value of the assets of a company or a security may have little or no significant relationship to market value.

BROKER: An agent, often a member of a stock exchange firm or an exchange member himself, who handles the public's orders to buy and sell securities or commodities. For this service a commission is charged. (See: *Commission, Commission Broker, Dealer*)

BROKERS' LOANS: Money borrowed by brokers from banks for a variety of uses. It may be used by specialists and odd-lot dealers to help finance inventories of stocks they deal in; by brokerage firms to finance the underwriting of new issues of corporate and municipal securities; to help finance a firm's own investments; and to help finance the purchase of securities for customers who prefer to use the broker's credit when they buy securities. (See: *Call Loan, Customers' Net Debit Balances, Margin*)

BUCKET SHOP: An illegal operation now almost extinct. The bucket-shop operator accepted a client's money without ever actually buying or selling securities as the client ordered. Instead he held the money and gambled that the customer was wrong. When too many customers were right, the bucket shop closed its doors and opened a new office.

BULL: One who believes the market will rise. (See: *Bear*)

BULL MARKET: An advancing market. (See: *Bear Market*)

CALL: (See: *Puts and Calls*)

CALL LOAN: A loan which may be terminated or "called" at any time by the lender or borrower. Used to finance purchases of securities. (See: *Broker's Loan*)

CALLABLE: A bond issue, all or part of which may be redeemed by the issuing corporation under definite conditions before maturity. The term also applies to preferred shares which may be redeemed by the issuing corporation.

CAPITAL GAIN OR CAPITAL LOSS: Profit or loss from the sale of a capital asset. A capital gain, under current federal income tax laws, may be either short-term (6 months or less) or long-term (more than 6 months). A short-term capital gain is taxed at the reporting individual's full income tax rate. A long-term capital gain is taxed at a maximum of 25 percent, depending on the reporting individual's tax bracket. Up to $1,000 of net capital loss—that is, when you sell securities at a lower price than you paid for them—is deductible from the individual's taxable income during the year reported. If the capital loss is more than $1,000, as much as $1,000 annually is deductible annually thereafter until all of the loss has been deducted. The amount of capital loss which may be deducted is reduced by the amount of any capital gain.

CAPITAL STOCK: All shares representing ownership of a business, including preferred and common. (See: *Common Stock, Preferred Stock*)

CAPITALIZATION: Total amount of the various securities issued by a corporation. Capitalization may include bonds, debentures, preferred and common stock. Bonds and debentures are usually carried on the books of the issuing company in terms of their par or face value. Preferred and common shares may be carried in terms of par or stated value. Stated value may be an arbitrary figure decided upon by the directors or may represent the amount received by the company from the sale of the securities at the time of issuance. (See: *Par*)

CASH FLOW: Reported net income of a corporation *plus* amounts charged off for depreciation, depletion, amortization, extraordinary charges to reserves, which are bookkeeping deductions and not paid out in actual dollars and cents. A yardstick used in recent years because of the larger noncash deductions appearing to offer a better indication of the ability of a company to pay dividends and finance expansion from self-generated cash than the conventional reported net income figure. (See: *Amortization, Depletion, Depreciation*)

CASH SALE: A transaction on the floor of the stock exchange which calls for delivery of the securities the same day. In "regular way" trades, the seller is allowed four business days for delivery. (See: *Regular-Way Delivery*)

CERTIFICATE: The actual piece of paper which is evidence of ownership of stock in a corporation. Watermarked paper is finely engraved with delicate etchings to discourage forgery. Loss of a certificate may at the least cause a great deal of inconvenience—at the worst, financial loss.

CLOSED-END INVESTMENT TRUST: (See: *Investment Trust*)

COLLATERAL: Securities or other property pledged by a borrower to secure repayment of a loan.

COLLATERAL TRUST BOND: A bond secured by collateral deposited with a trustee. The collateral is often the stocks or bonds of companies controlled by the issuing company but may be other securities.

COMMISSION: The broker's fee for purchasing or selling securities or property for a client. On the New York Stock Exchange the average commission is about 1 percent of the market value of the stocks involved in the transaction and approximately .025 percent on bonds.

COMMISSION BROKER: An agent who executes the public's orders for the purchase or sale of securities or commodities. (See: *Broker, Dealer*)

COMMON STOCK: Securities which represent an ownership interest in a corporation. If the company has also issued preferred stock, both common and preferred have ownership rights, but the preferred normally has prior claim on dividends and, in the event of liquidation, assets. Claims of both common and preferred stockholders are junior to claims of bondholders or other creditors of the company. Common stockholders assume the greater risk, but generally exercise the greater control and may gain the greater reward in the form of dividends and capital appreciation. The terms common stock and capital stock are often used interchangeably when the company has no preferred stock. (See: *Capital Stock, Preferred Stock*)

CONSOLIDATED BALANCE SHEET: A balance sheet showing the financial condition of a corporation and its subsidiaries. (See: *Balance Sheet*)

CONVERTIBLE: A bond, debenture, or preferred share which may be exchanged by the owner for common stock or another security, usually of the same company, in accordance with the terms of the issue.

CORNER: Buying of a stock or commodity on a scale large enough to give the buyer, or buying group, control over the price. A person who must buy that stock or commodity, for example one who is "short," is forced to do business at an arbitrarily high price with those who engineered the corner. (See: *Short Position, Short Sale*)

CORRESPONDENT: A securities firm, bank, or other financial organization which regularly performs services for another in a place or market to which the other does not have direct access. Securities firms may have correspondents in foreign countries or on exchanges of which they are not members. Correspondents are frequently linked by private wires. Member organizations with offices in New York City also act as correspondents for out-of-town member organizations which do not maintain New York City offices.

COUPON BOND: Bond with interest coupons attached. The coupons are clipped as they come due and are presented by the holder for payment of interest. (See: *Bearer Bond, Registered Bond*)

COVERING: Buying a security previously sold short. (See: *Short Sale, Short Covering*)

CUMULATIVE PREFERRED: A stock having a provision that if one or more dividends are omitted, the omitted dividends must be paid before dividends may be paid on the company's common stock.

CUMULATIVE VOTING: A method of voting for corporate directors which enables the shareholder to multiply the number of shares by the number of directorships being voted on and cast the total for one director or a selected group of directors. A 10-share holder normally casts 10 votes for each of, say 12 nominees to the board of directors. He thus has 120 votes. Under the cumulative voting principle he may do that or he may cast 120 (10x12) votes for only one nominee, 60 for two, 40 for three, or any other distribution he chooses. Cumulative voting is required under the corporate laws of some states, is permissive in most others.

CURB EXCHANGE: Former name of the American Stock Exchange, second largest exchange in the country. The term comes from the market's origin on the streets of downtown New York.

THE LANGUAGE OF INVESTING ⚜ ⚜ ⚜

CURRENT ASSETS: Those assets of a company which are reasonably expected to be realized in cash, or sold, or consumed during the normal operating cycle of the business. These include cash, U.S. Government bonds, receivables and money due usually within one year, and inventories.

CURRENT LIABILITIES: Money owed and payable by a company, usually within one year.

CURRENT RETURN: (See: *Yield*)

CUSTOMERS' MAN: (See: *Registered Representative*)

CUSTOMERS' NET DEBIT BALANCES: Credit of New York Stock Exchange member firms made available to help finance customers' purchases of stocks, bonds, and commodities.

DAY ORDER: On order to buy or sell which, if not executed, expires at the end of the trading day on which it was entered.

DEALER: An individual or firm in the securities business acting as a principal rather than as an agent. Typically, a dealer buys for his own account and sells to a customer from his own inventory. The dealer's profit or loss is the difference between the price he pays and the price he receives for the same security. The dealer's confirmation must disclose to his customer that he has acted as principal. The same individual or firm may function, at different times, either as broker or dealer. (See: *NASD, Specialist*)

DEBENTURE: A promissory note backed by the general credit of a company and usually not secured by a mortgage or lien on any specific property. (See: *Bond*)

DELIVERY: The certificate representing shares bought "regular way" on the New York Stock Exchange normally is delivered to the purchaser's broker on the fourth business day after the transaction. If a seller wants to delay delivery of the certificates, he may have his broker offer the stock "seller's option," instead of "regular way," and he may specify the number of days, from 5 up to 60, for delivery. A stock offered "seller's option" may command a lesser price than if offered "regular way." (See: *Bid and Asked, Cash Sale, Offer, Transfer*)

DEPLETION: Natural resources, such as metals, oils and gas, timber, which conceivably can be reduced to zero over the years, present a special problem in capital management. Deple-

193

tion is an accounting practice consisting of charges against earnings based upon the amount of the asset taken out of the total reserves in the period for which accounting is made. A bookkeeping entry, it does not represent any cash outlay nor any funds earmarked for the purpose.

DEPRECIATION: Normally, charges against earnings to write off the cost, less salvage value, of an asset over its estimated useful life. It is a bookkeeping entry and does not represent any cash outlay or are any funds earmarked for the purpose.

DIRECTOR: Person elected by shareholders at the annual meeting to establish company policies. The directors appoint the president, vice-presidents, and all other operating officers. Directors decide, among other matters, if and when dividends shall be paid. (See: *Management, Proxy*)

DISCRETIONARY ACCOUNT: An account in which the customer gives the broker or someone else discretion, which may be complete or within specific limits, as to the purchase and sales of securities or commodities including selection, timing, and price to be paid or received.

DISCRETIONARY ORDER: The customer empowers the broker to act on his behalf with respect to the choice of security to be bought or sold, the total amount of any securities to be bought or sold, and/or whether any such transaction shall be one of purchase or sale.

DISTRIBUTION: Selling of a large block of stock to a large group of investors. (See: *Exchange Distribution, Liquidation, Primary Distribution, Secondary Distribution, Special Offering*)

DIVERSIFICATION: Spreading investments among different companies in different fields. Another type of diversification is also offered by the securities of many individual companies because of the wide range of their activities. (See: *Investment Trust*)

DIVIDEND: The payment designated by the board of directors to be distributed pro rata among the shares outstanding. On preferred shares, it is generally a fixed amount. On common shares, the dividend varies with the fortunes of the company and the amount of cash on hand, and may be omitted if business is poor or the directors determine to withhold earnings to invest in plant and equipment. Sometimes a company will pay a dividend out of past earnings even if it is not currently operating at a profit.

DOLLAR-COST AVERAGING: A system of buying securities at regular intervals with a fixed dollar amount. Under this system the investor buys by the dollars' worth rather than by the number of shares. If each investment is of the same number of dollars, payments buy more when the price is low and fewer when it rises. Thus temporary downswings in price benefit the investor if he continues periodic purchases in both good times and bad and the price at which the shares are sold is more than their average cost. (See: *Formula Investing*)

DO-NOT-REDUCE (DNR) ORDER: A limited order to buy, a stop order to sell or a stop-limit order to sell which is not to be reduced by the amount of an ordinary cash dividend on the ex-dividend date. A do-not-reduce order applies only to ordinary cash dividends; it is reduced for other distributions such as a stock dividend or rights.

DOUBLE TAXATION: Short for double taxation of dividends. The federal government taxes corporate profits once as corporate income; any part of the remaining profits distributed as dividends to stockholders is taxed again as income to the recipient stockholder.

DOW THEORY: A theory of market analysis based upon the performance of the Dow-Jones industrial- and rail-stock price averages. The theory says that the market is in a basic upward trend if one of these averages advances above a previous important high, accompanied or followed by a similar advance in the other. When the averages both dip below previous important lows, this is regarded as confirmation of a basic downward trend. The theory does not attempt to predict how long either trend will continue, although it is widely misinterpreted as a method of forecasting future action. Whatever the merits of the theory, it is sometimes a strong factor in the market because many people believe in the theory—or believe that a great many others do. (See: *Technical Position*)

DOWN TICK: (See: *Up Tick*)

EARNINGS REPORT: A statement—also called an income statement—issued by a company showing its earnings or losses over a given period. The earnings report lists the income earned, expenses, and the net result. (See: *Balance Sheet*)

EQUIPMENT TRUST CERTIFICATE: A type of security, generally issued by a railroad, to pay for new equipment. Title to the equipment, such as a locomotive, is held by a trustee until the notes are paid off. An equipment trust certificate is usually secured by a first claim on the equipment.

EQUITY: The ownership interest of common and preferred stockholders in a company. Also refers to excess of value of securities over the debit balance in a margin account.

EXCHANGE ACQUISITION: A method of filling an order to buy a large block of stock on the floor of the exchange. Under certain circumstances, a member-broker can facilitate the purchase of a block by soliciting orders to sell. All orders to sell the security are lumped together and crossed with the buy order in the regular auction market. The price to the buyer may be on a net basis or on a commission basis.

EXCHANGE DISTRIBUTION: A method of disposing of large blocks of stock on the floor of the exchange. Under certain circumstances, a member-broker can facilitate the sale of a block of stock by soliciting and getting other member-brokers to solicit orders to buy. Individual buy orders are lumped together and crossed with the sell order in the regular auction market. A special commission is usually paid by the seller; ordinarily the buyer pays no commission.

EX-DIVIDEND: A synonym for "without dividend." The buyer of a stock selling ex-dividend does not receive the recently declared dividend. Open buy-and-sell stop orders, and sell stop-limit orders in a stock on the ex-dividend date are ordinarily reduced by the value of that dividend. In the case of open stop-limit orders to sell, both the stop price and the limit price are reduced. Every dividend is payable on a fixed date to all shareholders recorded on the books of the company as of a previous date of record. For example, a dividend may be declared as payable to holders of record on the books of the company on a given Friday. Since four business days are allowed for delivery of stock in a "regular way" transaction on the New York Stock Exchange, the exchange would declare the stock "ex-dividend" as of the opening of the market on the preceding Tuesday. That means anyone who bought it on and after Tuesday would not be entitled to that dividend. (See: *Cash Sale, Delivery, Net Change, Transfer*)

Ex-Rights: Without the rights. Corporations raising additional money may do so by offering their stockholders the right to subscribe to new or additional stock, usually at a discount from the prevailing market price. The buyer of a stock selling ex-rights is not entitled to the rights. (See: *Ex-Dividend, Rights*)

Extra: The short form of "extra dividend." A dividend in the form of stock or cash in addition to the regular or usual dividend the company has been paying.

Face Value: The value of a bond that appears on the face of the bond, unless the value is otherwise specified by the issuing company. Face value is ordinarily the amount the issuing company promises to pay at maturity. Face value is not an indication of market value. Sometimes referred to as par value.

Fill or Kill: A market or limited-price order is to be executed in its entirety as soon as it is represented in the trading crowd. If not so executed, the order is treated as canceled. For purposes of this definition, a "stop" (See: *Stopped Stock*) is considered an execution.

Fiscal Year: A corporation's accounting year. Due to the nature of their particular business, some companies do not use the calendar year for their bookkeeping. A typical example is the department store which finds December 31 too early a date to close its books after the Christmas rush. For that reason many stores wind up their accounting year January 31. Their fiscal year, therefore, runs from February 1 of one year through January 31 of the next. The fiscal year of other companies may run from July 1 through the following June 30. Most companies, though, operate on a calendar year basis.

Fixed Charges: A company's fixed expenses, such as bond interest, which it has agreed to pay whether or not earned, and which are deducted from income before earnings on equity capital are computed.

Flat: This term means that the price at which a bond is traded includes consideration for all unpaid accruals of interest. Bonds which are in default of interest or principal are traded flat. Income bonds, which pay interest only to the extent earned, are usually traded flat. All other bonds are usually dealt in "and interest," which means that the buyer pays to the seller the market price plus interest accrued since the last payment date.

When applied to a stock loan, flat means without premium or interest. (See: *Short Sale*)

FLOOR: The huge trading area—about two-thirds the size of a football field—where stocks and bonds are bought and sold on the New York Stock Exchange.

FLOOR BROKER: A member of the Stock Exchange who executes orders on the floor of the exchange to buy or sell any listed securities. (See: *Commission Broker, Two-Dollar Broker*)

FLOOR TRADER: (See: *Registered Trader*)

FLUCTUATION: (See: *Point*)

FORMULA INVESTING: An investment technique. One formula calls for the shifting of funds from common shares to preferred shares or bonds as the market, on average, rises above a certain predetermined point—and the return of funds to common-share investments as the market average declines. (See: *Dollar Cost Averaging*)

FREE AND OPEN MARKET: A market in which supply and demand are expressed in terms of price. Contrasts with a controlled market in which supply, demand, and price may all be regulated.

FUNDED DEBT: Usually interest-bearing bonds or debentures of a company. Could include long-term bank loans. Does *not* include short-term loans, preferred or common stock.

GENERAL MORTGAGE BOND: A bond which is secured by a blanket mortgage on the company's property, but which is often outranked by one or more other mortgages.

GILT-EDGED: High-grade bond issued by a company which has demonstrated its ability to earn a comfortable profit over a period of years and pay its bondholders their interest without interruption.

GIVE UP: A term with two different meanings. For one, a member of the exchange on the floor may act for a second member by executing an order for him with a third member. The first member tells the third member that he is acting on behalf of the second member and gives the second member's name rather than his own. For another, if you have an account with Doe & Company but you're in a town where Doe has no office, you go to another member firm, tell them you have an account with Doe & Company and would like to buy some stock. After verifying your account with Doe & Company, the firm may execute your order and tell the broker who sells the stock that the firm is acting on behalf of Doe & Company. They give up the name of Doe & Company to the selling broker. Or the firm may simply wire your order to Doe & Company who will execute it for you. In either case you pay only the regular commission.

GOOD DELIVERY: Certain basic qualifications must be met before a security sold on the exchange may be delivered. The security must be in proper form to comply with the contract of sale and to transfer title by delivery to the purchaser.

GOOD-'TIL-CANCELED ORDER (GTC) OR OPEN ORDER: An order to buy or sell which remains in effect until it is either executed or canceled.

GOVERNMENT BONDS: Obligations of the U.S. Government, regarded as the highest grade issues in existence.

GROWTH STOCK: Stock of a company with prospects for future growth—a company whose earnings are expected to increase at a relatively rapid rate.

GUARANTEED BOND: A bond which has interest or principal, or both, guaranteed by a company other than the issuer. Usually found in the railroad industry when large roads, leasing sections of trackage owned by small railroads, may guarantee the bonds of the smaller road.

GUARANTEED STOCK: Usually preferred stock on which dividends are guaranteed by another company under much the same circumstances as a bond is guaranteed.

HEDGE: (See: *Arbitrage, Puts & Calls, Selling Against the Box, Short Sale*)

HOLDING COMPANY: A corporation which owns the securities of another, in most cases with voting control.

HYPOTHECATION: The pledging of securities as collateral for a loan.

IMMEDIATE OR CANCEL ORDER: A market or limited-price order which is to be executed in whole or in part as soon as it is represented in the trading crowd, and the portion not so executed is to be treated as canceled. For the purposes of this definition, a "stop" is considered an execution. (See: *Stopped Stock*)

INACTIVE POST: A trading post on the floor of the New York Stock Exchange where inactive securities are traded in units of 10 shares instead of the usual 100-share lots. Better known in the business as Post 30. (See: *Round Lot*)

INACTIVE STOCK: An issue traded on an exchange or in the over-the-counter market in which there is a relatively low volume of transactions. Volume may be no more than a few hundred shares a week or even less. On the New York Stock Exchange many inactive stocks are traded in 10-share units rather than the customary 100. (See: *Round Lot*)

IN-AND-OUT: Purchase and sale of the same security within a short period—a day, a week, even a month. An in-and-out trader is generally more interested in day-to-day price fluctuations than dividends or long-term growth.

INCOME BOND: Generally income bonds promise to repay principal but to pay interest only when earned. In some cases unpaid interest on an income bond may accumulate as a claim against the corporation when the bond becomes due. (See: *Bond, Collateral Trust Bond, Convertible, General Mortgage Bond*)

INDENTURE: A written agreement under which debt securities are issued, setting forth maturity date, interest rate, security, and other terms.

INDEX: A statistical yardstick expressed in terms of percentages of a base year or years. For instance, the Federal Reserve Board's index of industrial production is based on 1957-59 as 100. In September, 1965, the index stood at 142.8, which means that industrial production that month was 42.8 percent higher than in the base period. An index is not an average. (See: *Averages*)

INTEREST: Payments a borrower pays a lender for the use of his money. A corporation pays interest on its bonds to its bondholders. (See: *Bond, Dividend*)

INVESTMENT: The use of money for the purpose of making more money, to gain income or increase capital, or both. Safety of principal is an important consideration. (See: *Speculation*)

200

INVESTMENT BANKER: Also known as an underwriter. He is the middleman between the corporation issuing new securities and the public. The usual practice is for one or more investment bankers to buy outright from a corporation a new issue of stocks or bonds. The group forms a syndicate to sell the securities to individuals and institutions. Investment bankers also distribute very large blocks of stocks or bonds—perhaps held by an estate. Thereafter the market in the security may be over-the-counter, on a regional stock exchange, the American Exchange or the New York Stock Exchange. (See: *Over-the-Counter, Primary Distribution, Syndicate*)

INVESTMENT COUNSEL: One whose principal business consists of acting as investment advisor and a substantial part of his business consists of rendering investment supervisory services.

INVESTMENT TRUST: A company which uses its capital to invest in other companies. There are two principal types: the closed-end and the open-end, or mutual fund. Shares in closed-end investment trusts, some of which are listed on the New York Stock Exchange, are readily transferable in the open market and are bought and sold like other shares. Capitalization of these companies remains the same unless action is taken to change, which is seldom. Open-end funds sell their own new shares to investors, stand ready to buy back their old shares, and are not listed. Open-end funds are so-called because their capitalization is not fixed; they issue more shares as people want them.

INVESTOR: An individual whose principal concerns in the purchase of a security are regular dividend income, safety of the original investment, and, if possible, capital appreciation. (See: *Speculator*)

ISSUE: Any of a company's securities, or the act of distributing such securities.

LEGAL LIST: A list of investments selected by various states in which certain institutions and fiduciaries, such as insurance companies and banks, may invest. Legal lists are restricted to high quality securities meeting certain specifications. (See: *Prudent Man Rule*)

LEVERAGE: The effect on the per-share earnings of the common stock of a company when large sums must be paid for bond interest or preferred stock dividends, or both, before the common stock is entitled to share in earnings. Leverage may be advantageous for the common when earnings are good but may work against the common stock when earnings decline. Example: Company A has 1,000,000 shares of common stock outstanding, no other securities. Earnings drop from $1,000,000 to $800,000 or from $1 to 80 cents a share, a decline of 20 percent. Company B also has 1,000,000 shares of common but must pay $500,000 annually in bond interest. If earnings amount to $1,000,000, there is $500,000 available for the common or 50 cents a share. But earnings drop to $800,000 so there is only $300,000 available for the common, or 30 cents a share—a drop of 40 percent. Or suppose earnings of the company with only common stock increased from $1,000,000 to $1,500,000—earnings per share would go from $1 to $1.50, or an increase of 50 percent. But if earnings of the company which had to pay $500,000 in bond interest increased that much—earnings per common share would jump from 50 cents to $1 a share, or 100 percent. When a company has common stock only, no leverage exists because all earnings are available for the common, although relatively large fixed charges payable for lease of substantial plant assets may have an effect similar to that of a bond issue.

LIABILITIES: All the claims against a corporation. Liabilities include accounts and wages and salaries payable, dividends declared payable, accrued taxes payable, fixed or long-term liabilities such as mortgage bonds, debentures and bank loans. (See: *Assets, Balance Sheet*)

LIEN: A claim against property which has been pledged or mortgaged to secure the performance of an obligation. A bond is usually secured by a lien against specified property of a company. (See: *Bond*)

LIMIT, LIMITED ORDER, OR LIMITED-PRICE ORDER: An order to buy or sell a stated amount of a security at a specified price, or at a better price, if obtainable after the order is represented in the trading crowd.

LIQUIDATION: The process of converting securities or other property into cash. The dissolution of a company, with cash remaining after sale of its assets and payments of all indebtedness being distributed to the shareholders.

LIQUIDITY: The ability of the market in a particular security to absorb a reasonable amount of buying or selling at reasonable price changes. Liquidity is one of the most important characteristics of a good market.

THE LANGUAGE OF INVESTING ✤ ✤ ✤

LISTED STOCK: The stock of a company which is traded on a securities exchange, and for which a listing application and a registration statement, giving detailed information about the company and its operations, have been filed with the Securities & Exchange Commission, unless otherwise exempted, and the exchange itself. The various stock exchanges have different standards for listing. Some of the guides used by the New York Stock Exchange for an original listing are national interest in the company, a minimum of 1 million shares outstanding with at least 700 thousand shares publicly held among not less than 2,000 shareholders including at least 1,700 round-lot stockholders. The publicly held common shares should have a minimum aggregate market value of $12 million. Normally the company should have earning power of over $2 million annually before taxes and of over $1.2 million after all charges and taxes.

LOAD: The portion of the offering price of shares of open-end investment companies which covers sales commissions and all other costs of distribution. The load is incurred only on purchase, there being, in most cases, no charge when the shares are sold (redeemed).

LOCKED IN: An investor is said to be locked in when he has a profit on a security he owns but does not sell because his profit would immediately become subject to the capital gains tax. (See: *Capital Gain*)

LONG: Signifies ownership of securities. "I am long 100 U. S. Steel" means the speaker owns 100 shares. (See: *Short Position, Short Sale*)

MANAGEMENT: The board of directors, elected by the stockholders, and the officers of the corporation, appointed by the board of directors.

MANIPULATION: An illegal operation. Buying or selling a security for the purpose of creating false or misleading appearance of active trading or for the purpose of raising or depressing the price to induce purchase or sale by others.

MARGIN: The amount paid by the customer when he uses his broker's credit to buy a security. Under Federal Reserve regulations, the initial margin required in the past 20 years has ranged from 40 percent of the purchase price all the way to 100 percent. (See: *Brokers' Loans, Equity, Margin Call*)

203

MARGIN CALL: A demand upon a customer to put up money or securities with the broker. The call is made when a purchase is made; also if a customer's equity in a margin account declines below a minimum standard set by the exchange or by the firm. (See: *Margin*)

MARKET ORDER: An order to buy or sell a stated amount of a security at the most advantageous price obtainable after the order is represented in the trading crowd. (See: *Good-'til-Canceled Order, Limit Order, Stop Order*)

MARKET PRICE: In the case of a security, market price is usually considered the last reported price at which the stock or bond sold.

MATCHED AND LOST: When two bids to buy the same stock are made on the trading floor simultaneously, and each bid is equal to or larger than the amount of stock offered, both bids are considered to be on an equal basis. So the two bidders flip a coin to decide who buys the stock. Also applies to offers to sell.

MATURITY: The date on which a loan or a bond or debenture comes due and is to be paid off.

MEMBER CORPORATION: A securities brokerage firm, organized as a corporation, with at least one member of the New York Stock Exchange who is a director and a holder of voting stock in the corporation. (See: *Member Firm*)

MEMBER FIRM: A securities brokerage firm organized as a partnership and having at least one general partner who is a member of the New York Stock Exchange. (See: *Member Corporation*)

MEMBER ORGANIZATION: This term includes New York Stock Exchange member firms and member corporations. The term "participant" when used with reference to a member organization includes general and limited partners of a member firm and holders of voting and nonvoting stock in a member corporation. (See: *Member Corporation, Member Firm*)

MIP: Monthly Investment Plan. A pay-as-you-go method of buying New York Stock Exchange listed shares on a regular payment plan for as little as $40 a month, or $40 every three months. Under MIP the investor buys stock by the dollars' worth—if the price advances, he gets fewer shares and if it declines, he gets more shares. He may discontinue purchases at any time without penalty. The commission ranges from 6 percent on small transactions to slightly below 1½ percent on larger transactions. (See: *Dollar-Cost Averaging, Odd-Lot Dealer*)

MORTGAGE BOND: A bond secured by a mortgage on a property. The value of the property may or may not equal the value of the so-called mortgage bonds issued against it. (See: *Bond, Debenture*)

MUNICIPAL BOND: A bond issued by a state or a political subdivision, such as county, city, town, or village. The term also designates bonds issued by state agencies and authorities. In general, interest paid on municipal bonds is exempt from federal income taxes.

MUTUAL FUND: (See: *Investment Trust*)

NASD: The National Association of Securities Dealers, Inc., an association of brokers and dealers in the over-the-counter securities business. The association has the power to expel members who have been determined guilty of unethical practices. NASD is dedicated to—among other objectives—"adopt, administer, and enforce rules of fair practice and rules to prevent fraudulent and manipulative acts and practices, and in general to promote just and equitable principles of trade for the protection of investors."

NEGOTIABLE: Refers to a security, title to which is transferable by delivery. (See: *Delivery, Good Delivery*)

NET ASSET VALUE: A term usually used in connection with investment trust, meaning net-asset value per share. It is common practice for an investment trust to compute its assets daily, or even twice daily, by totaling the market value of all securities owned. All liabilities are deducted, and the balance divided by the number of shares outstanding. The resulting figure is the net-asset value per share (See: *Assets, Investment Trust*)

NET CHANGE: The change in the price of a security from the closing price on one day and the closing price on the following day on which the stock is traded. In the case of a stock which is entitled to a dividend one day, but is traded "ex-dividend" the next, the dividend is considered in computing the change. For

205

example, if the closing market price of a stock on Monday—the last day it was entitled to receive a 50-cent dividend—was $45 a share, and $44.50 at the close of the next day, when it was "ex-dividend," the price would be considered unchanged. The same applies to a split-up of shares. A stock selling at $100 the day before a 2-for-1 split and trading the next day at $50 would be considered unchanged. If it sold at $51, it would be considered up $1. The net change is ordinarily the last figure in a stock price list. The mark +1⅛ means up $1.125 a share from the last sale on the previous day the stock traded. (See: *Ex-Dividend, Point, Split*)

NEW ISSUE: A stock or bond sold by a corporation for the first time. Proceeds may be issued to retire outstanding securities of the company, for new plant or equipment or for additional working capital.

NONCUMULATIVE: A preferred stock on which unpaid dividends do not accrue. Omitted dividends are, as a rule, gone forever. (See: *Cumulative Preferred*)

"NOT HELD" ORDER: A market or limited price order marked "not held," "disregard tape," "take time," or which bears any such qualifying notation. An order marked "or better" is not a "not held" order.

ODD LOT: An amount of stock less than the established 100-share unit or 10-share unit of trading: from 1 to 99 shares for the great majority of issues, 1 to 9 for so-called inactive stocks. (See: *Round Lot, Inactive Stock*)

ODD-LOT DEALER: A member firm of the exchange which buys and sells odd lots of stocks—1 to 9 shares in the case of stocks traded in 10-share units and 1 to 99 shares for 100-share units. The odd-lot dealer's customers are commission brokers acting on behalf of their customers. There are one or more odd-lot dealers ready to buy or sell, for their own accounts, odd lots in any stock at any time. There are at least 4 representatives of odd-lot dealers at each of the 18 active trading posts on the floor of the New York Stock Exchange. Odd-lot prices are geared to the auction market. On an odd-lot market order, the odd-lot dealer's price is based on the first round-lot transaction which occurs on the floor following receipt at the trading post of the odd-lot order. The usual differential between the odd-lot price and the "effective" round-lot price is 12½ cents a share for stock selling below $40 and 25 cents a share for stock at $40 or more. For example: You decide to buy 20 shares of ABC common at the market. Your order is transmitted by your commission broker to the representative of an odd-lot dealer at the post where ABC is traded. A few minutes later there is a 100-share transaction in ABC at $10 a share. The odd-lot price at which your order is immediately filled by the odd-lot dealer is $10.125 a share. If you had sold 20 shares of ABC, you would have received $9.875 a share. (See: *Commission Broker, Dealer, Inactive Stock, Round Lot, Transfer Tax*)

OFF-BOARD: This term may refer to transactions over-the-counter in unlisted securities, or, in a special situation, to a transaction involving listed shares which was not executed on a national securities exchange. (See: *Over-the-Counter, Secondary Distribution*)

OFFER: The price at which a person is ready to sell. Opposed to bid, the price at which one is ready to buy. (See: *Bid and Asked*)

OPEN-END INVESTMENT TRUST: (See: *Investment Trust*)

OPEN ORDER: (See: *Good-'til-Canceled Order*)

OPTION: A right to buy or sell specific securities or properties at a specified price within a specified time. (See: *Puts and Calls*)

ORDERS GOOD UNTIL A SPECIFIED TIME: A market or limited price order which is to be represented in the trading crowd until a specified time, after which such order or the portion thereof not executed is to be treated as canceled.

OVERBOUGHT: An opinion as to price levels. May refer to a security which has had a sharp rise or to the market as a whole after a period of vigorous buying which, it may be argued, has left prices "too high." (See: *Technical Position*)

OVERSOLD: An opinion—the reverse of overbought. A single security or a market which, it is believed, has declined to an unreasonable level. (See: *Technical Position*)

OVER-THE-COUNTER: A market for securities made up of securities dealers who may or may not be members of a securities exchange. Over-the-counter is mainly a market made over the telephone. Thousands of companies have insufficient shares out-standing, stockholders, or earnings to warrant application for listing on a stock exchange. Securities of these companies are traded in the over-the-counter market between dealers who act either as principals or as brokers for customers. The over-the-counter market is the principal market for U.S. Government bonds and municipals. (See: *NASD, Off-Board*)

PAPER PROFIT: An unrealized profit on a security still held. Paper profits become realized profits only when the security is sold.

PAR: In the case of a common share, par means a dollar amount assigned to the share by the company's charter. Par value may also be used to compute the dollar amount of the common shares on the balance sheet. Par value has little significance today so far as market value of common stock is concerned. Many companies today issue no-par stock but give a stated per-share value on the balance sheet. Par at one time was supposed to represent the value of the original investment behind each share in cash, goods, or services. In the case of preferred shares and bonds, however, par still is important. It often signifies the dollar value upon which dividends on preferred stocks, and interest on bonds, are figured. The issuer of a 3 percent bond promises to pay that percentage of the bond's par value annually. (See: *Capitalization, Transfer Tax*)

PARTICIPATING PREFERRED: A preferred stock which is entitled to its stated dividend and, also, to additional dividends on a specified basis upon payment of dividends on the common stock.

PASSED DIVIDEND: Omission of a regular or scheduled dividend.

PENNY STOCKS: Low-priced issues often highly speculative, selling at less than $1 a share. Frequently used as a term of disparagement, although a few penny stocks have developed into investment-caliber issues.

PERCENTAGE ORDER: A market or limited price order to buy (or sell) a stated amount of a specified stock after a fixed number of shares of such stock have traded.

POINT: In the case of shares of stock, a point means $1. If General Motors shares rise 3 points, each share has risen $3. In the case of bonds a point means $10, since a bond is quoted as a percentage of $1,000. A bond which rises 3 points gains 3 percent of $1,000 or $30 in value. An advance from 87 to 90 would mean an advance in dollar value from $870 to $900 for each $1,000 bond. In the case of market averages, the word point means merely that and no more. If, for example, the Dow-Jones industrial average rises from 950.25 to 951.25, it has risen a point. A point in the averages, however, is not equivalent to $1. (See: *Averages*)

PORTFOLIO: Holdings of securities by an individual or institution. A portfolio may contain bonds, preferred stocks, and common stocks of various types of enterprises.

PREFERRED STOCK: A class of stock with a claim on the company's earnings before payment may be made on the common stock and usually entitled to priority over common stock if the company liquidates. Usually entitled to dividends at a specified rate—when declared by the board of directors and before payment of a dividend on the common stock—depending upon the terms of the issue. (See: *Cumulative Preferred, Participating Preferred*)

PREMIUM: The amount by which a preferred stock or bond may sell above its par value. In the case of a new issue of bonds or stocks, premium is the amount the market price rises over the original selling price. Also refers to a charge sometimes made when a stock is borrowed to make delivery on a short sale. May refer, also, to redemption price of a bond or preferred stock if it is higher than face value. (See: *Corner, Short Sale*)

PRICE-EARNINGS RATIO: The current market price of a share of stock divided by earnings per share for a 12-month period. For example, a stock selling for $100 a share and earning $5 a share is said to be selling at a price-earnings ratio of 20 to 1.

PRIMARY DISTRIBUTION: Also called primary offering. The original sale of a company's securities. (See: *Investment Banker, Secondary Distribution*)

PRINCIPAL: The person for whom a broker executes an order, or a dealer buying or selling for his own account. The term "principal" may also refer to a person's capital or to the face amount of a bond.

PRIOR PREFERRED: A preferred stock which usually takes precedence over other preferreds issued by the same company.

PROFIT TAKING: Selling to take a profit, the process of converting paper profits into cash.

PROSPECTUS: A circular which describes securities being offered for sale to the public. Required by the Securities Act of 1933.

PROXY: Written authorization given by a shareholder to someone else to represent him and vote his shares at a shareholders' meeting.

PROXY STATEMENT: Information required by SEC to be given stockholders as a prerequisite to solicitation of proxies for a security subject to the requirements of the Securities Exchange Act.

PRUDENT MAN RULE: An investment standard. In some states, the law requires that a fiduciary, such as a trustee, may invest the fund's money only in a list of securities designated by the state—the so-called legal list. In other states, the trustee may invest in a security if it is one which a prudent man of discretion and intelligence, who is seeking a reasonable income and preservation of capital, would buy.

PUTS AND CALLS: Options which give the right to buy or sell a fixed amount of a certain stock at a specified price within a specified time. A put gives the holder the right to sell the stock; a call the right to buy the stock. Puts are purchased by those who think a stock may go down. A put obligates the seller of the contract to take delivery of the stock and pay the specified price to the owner of the option within the time limit of the contract. The price specified in a put or call is usually close to the market price of the stock at the time the contract is made. Calls are purchased by those who think a stock may rise. A call gives the holder the right to buy the stock from the seller of the contract at the specified price within a fixed period of time. Put and call contracts are written for 30, 60, or 90 days, or longer. If the purchaser of a put or call does not wish to exercise the option, the price he paid for the option becomes a loss.

QUOTATION: Often shortened to "quote." The highest bid to buy and the lowest offer to sell a security in a given market at a given time. If you ask your broker for a "quote" on a stock, he may come back with something like "45¼ to 45½." This means that $45.25 is the highest price any buyer wanted to pay at the time the quote was given on the floor of the exchange and that $45.50 was the lowest price which any seller would take at the same time. (See: *Bid and Asked*)

RALLY: A brisk rise following a decline in the general price level of the market, or in an individual stock.

REALIZING: (See: *Profit Taking*)

RECORD DATE: The date on which you must be registered on the books of a company as a shareholder in order to receive a declared dividend or, among other things, to vote on company affairs. (See: *Delivery, Ex-Dividend, Transfer*)

REDEMPTION PRICE: The price at which a bond may be redeemed before maturity at the option of the issuing company. Redemption value also applies to the price the company must pay to call in certain types of preferred stock. (See: *Callable*)

REFINANCING: Same as refunding. New securities are sold by a company and the money is used to retire existing securities. Object may be to save interest costs, extend the maturity of the loan, or both.

REGISTERED BOND: A bond which is registered on the books of the issuing company in the name of the owner. It can be transferred only when endorsed by the registered owner. (See: *Bearer Bond, Coupon Bond*)

REGISTERED REPRESENTATIVE: Present name for the older term "customers' man." In a New York Stock Exchange member firm, a registered representative is a full-time employee who has met the requirements of the exchange as to background and knowledge of the securities business. Also known as an account executive or customer's broker.

REGISTERED TRADER: A member of the exchange who trades in stocks on the floor for an account in which he has an interest. (See: *Floor Trader*)

REGISTRAR: Usually a trust company or bank charged with the responsibility of preventing the issuance of more stock than authorized by a company. (See: *Transfer*)

REGISTRATION: Before a public offering may be made of new securities by a company, or of outstanding securities by controlling stockholders—through the mails or in interstate commerce

—the securities must be registered under the Securities Act of 1933. The registration statement is filed with the SEC by the issuer. It must disclose all pertinent information relating to the company's operations, securities, management, and purpose of the public offering. Securities of railroads under jurisdiction of the Interstate Commerce Commission, and certain other types of securities, are exempted. On security offerings involving less than $300,000, less information is required.

Before a security may be admitted to dealings on a national securities exchange, it must be registered under the Securities Exchange Act of 1934. The application for registration must be filed with the exchange and the SEC by the company issuing the securities. The application must disclose pertinent information relating to the company's operations, securities, and management. Registration may become effective 30 days after receipt by the SEC of the certification by the exchange of approval of listing and registration, or sooner by special order of the Commission.

REGULAR WAY DELIVERY: Unless otherwise specified, securities (other than governments) sold on the New York Stock Exchange are to be delivered to the buying broker by the selling broker and payment made to the selling broker by the buying broker on the fourth business day after the transaction. Regular way delivery for government bonds is the following business day. (See: *Delivery, Transfer*)

REGULATION T: The federal regulation governing the amount of credit which may be advanced by brokers and dealers to customers for the purchase of securities. (See: *Margin*)

REGULATION U: The federal regulation governing the amount of credit which may be advanced by a bank to its customers for the purchase of listed stocks. (See: *Margin*)

RETURN: (See: *Yield*)

RIGHTS: When a company wants to raise more funds by issuing additional securities, it may give its stockholders the opportunity, ahead of others, to buy the new securities in proportion to the number of shares each owns. The piece of paper evidencing this privilege is called a right. Because the additional stock is usually offered to stockholders below the current market price, rights ordinarily have a market value of their own and are actively traded. In most cases they must be exercised within a relatively short period. Failure to exercise or sell rights may result in actual loss to the holder. (See: *Warrant*)

ROUND LOT: A unit of trading or a multiple thereof. On the New York Stock Exchange the unit of trading is generally 100 shares in stocks and $1,000 par value in the case of bonds. In some inactive stocks, the unit of trading is 10 shares.

SCALE ORDER: An order to buy (or sell) a security which specifies the total amount to be bought (or sold) and the amount to be bought (or sold) at specified price variations.

SCRIP: A certificate exchangeable for stock or cash before a specified date, after which it may have no value. Usually issued for fractions of shares in connection with a stock dividend or split or in reorganization of a company. For example, a stock dividend might amount to only one-third share so scrip is issued instead of a stock certificate for one-third share. Not traded on New York Stock Exchange. (See: *Stock Dividend*)

SEAT: A traditional figure-of-speech for a membership on a securities or commodity exchange. Price and admission requirements vary.

SEC: The Securities and Exchange Commission, established by Congress to help protect investors. The SEC administers the Securities Act of 1933, the Securities Exchange Act of 1934, the Trust Indenture Act, the Investment Company Act, the Investment Advisers Act, and the Public Utility Holding Company Act.

SECONDARY DISTRIBUTION: Also known as a secondary offering. The redistribution of a block of stock some time after it has been sold by the issuing company. The sale is handled off the New York Stock Exchange by a securities firm or group of firms and the shares are usually offered at a fixed price which is related to the current market price of the stock. Usually the block is a large one, such as might be involved in the settlement of an estate. The security may be listed or unlisted. (See: *Exchange Distribution, Investment Banker, Primary Distribution, Special Offering, Syndicate*)

SELLER'S OPTION: A special transaction on the stock exchange which gives the seller the right to deliver the stock or bond at any time within a specified period, ranging from not less than 5 business days to not more than 60 days. (See: *Delivery*)

SELLING AGAINST THE BOX: A method of protecting a paper profit. Let's say you own 100 shares of XYZ which has advanced in price, and you think the price may decline. So you sell 100 shares short, borrowing 100 shares to make delivery. You retain in your security box the 100 shares which you own. If XYZ declines, the profit on your short sale is exactly offset by the loss in the market value of the stock you own. If XYZ advances, the loss on your short sale is exactly offset by the profit in the market value of the stock you have retained. You can close out your short sale by buying 100 shares to return to the person from whom you borrowed, or you can send them the 100 shares which you own. (See: *Hedge, Short Sale*)

SERIAL BOND: An issue which matures in relatively small amounts at periodic stated intervals.

SHORT COVERING: Buying stock to return stock previously borrowed to make delivery on a short sale.

SHORT POSITION: Stocks sold short and not covered as of a particular date. On the New York Stock Exchange, a tabulation is issued a few days after the middle of the month listing all issues on the exchange in which there was a short position of 5,000 or more shares, and issues in which the short position had changed by 2,000 or more shares in the preceding month. This tabulation is based on reports of positions on member firms' books. Short position also means the total amount of stock an individual has sold short and has not covered, as of a particular date. Initial margin requirements for a short position are the same as for a long position. (See: *Margin, Up Tick, Short Sale*)

SHORT SALE: A person who believes a stock will decline and sells it though he does not own any has made a short sale. For instance: You instruct your broker to sell short 100 shares of ABC. Your broker borrows the stock so he can deliver the 100 shares to the buyer. The money value of the shares borrowed is deposited by your broker with the lender. Sooner or later you must cover your short sale by buying the same amount of stock you borrowed for return to the lender. If you are able to buy ABC at a lower price than you sold it for, your profit is the difference between the two prices—not counting commissions and taxes. But if you have to pay more for the stock than the price you received, that is the amount of your loss. Stock exchange and federal regulations govern and limit the conditions under which a short sale may be made on a national securities exchange. (See: *Margin, Premium, Up Tick*)

SINKING FUND: Money regularly set aside by a company to redeem its bonds, debentures, or preferred stock from time to time as specified in the indenture or charter.

SPECIAL BID: A method of filling an order to buy a large block of stock on the floor of the New York Stock Exchange. In a special bid, the bidder for the block of stock—a pension fund, for instance, will pay a special commission to the broker who represents him in making the purchase. The seller does not pay a commission. The special bid is made on the floor of the exchange at a fixed price which may not be below the last sale of the security or the current bid in the regular market, whichever is higher. Member firms may sell this stock for customers directly to the buyer's broker during trading hours.

SPECIAL OFFERING: Occasionally a large block of stock becomes available for sale which, due to its size and the market in that particular issue, calls for special handling. A notice is printed on the ticker tape announcing that the stock will be offered for sale on the floor of the exchange at a fixed price. Member firms may buy this stock for customers directly from the seller's broker during trading hours. The price is usually based on the last transaction in the regular auction market. If there are more buyers than stock, allotments are made. Only the seller pays a commission on a special offering. (See: *Secondary Distribution*)

SPECIALIST: A member of the New York Stock Exchange who has two functions: First, to maintain an orderly market, insofar as reasonably practicable, in the stocks in which he is registered as a specialist. In order to maintain an orderly market, the exchange expects the specialist to buy or sell for his own account, to a reasonable degree, when there is a temporary disparity between supply and demand. Second, the specialist acts as a broker's broker. When a commission broker on the exchange floor receives a limit order, say, to buy at $50 a stock then selling at $60—he cannot wait at the particular post where the stock is traded until the price reaches the specified level. So he leaves the order with the specialist, who will try to execute it in the market if and when the stock declines to the specified price. At all times the specialist must put his customers' interests above his own. There are about 350 specialists on the New York Stock Exchange. (See: *Book, Limited Order*)

SPECIALIST BLOCK PURCHASE: Purchase by the specialist for his own account of a large block of stock outside the regular market on the exchange. Such purchases may be made only when the sale of the block could not be made in the regular market within a reasonable time and at reasonable prices, and when the purchase by the specialist would aid him in maintaining a fair and orderly market. The specialist need not fill the orders on his book down to the purchase price.

SPECIALIST BLOCK SALE: Opposite of the specialist block purchase. Under exceptional circumstances, the specialist may sell a block of stock outside the regular market on the exchange for his own account at a price above the prevailing market. The price is negotiated between the specialist and the broker for the buyer. The specialist need not fill the orders on his book up to the purchase price.

SPECULATION: The employment of funds by a speculator. Safety of principal is a secondary factor. (See: *Investment*)

SPECULATOR: One who is willing to assume a relatively large risk in the hope of gain. His principal concern is to increase his capital rather than his dividend income. The speculator may buy and sell the same day or speculate in an enterprise which he does not expect to be profitable for years. (See: *Investor*)

SPLIT: The division of the outstanding shares of a corporation into a larger number of shares. A 3-for-1 split by a company with 1 million shares outstanding would result in 3 million shares outstanding. Each holder of 100 shares before the 3-for-1 split would have 300 shares, although his proportionate equity in the company would remain the same, since 100 parts of 1 million are the equivalent of 300 parts of 3 million. Ordinarily splits must be voted by directors and approved by shareholders. (See: *Stock Dividend*)

STOCK AHEAD: Sometimes an investor who has entered an order to buy or sell a stock at a certain price will see transactions at that price reported on the ticker tape while his own order has not been executed. The reason is that other buy-and-sell orders at the same price came in to the specialist ahead of his and had priority. (See: *Book, Specialist*)

STOCK CLEARING CORPORATION: A subsidiary of the New York Stock Exchange which acts as a central agency for security deliveries and money payments between member firms of the exchange.

216

STOCK DIVIDEND: A dividend paid in securities rather than cash. The dividend may be additional shares of the issuing company, or in shares of another company (usually a subsidiary) held by the company. (See: *Ex-Dividend, Split*)

STOCKHOLDER OF RECORD: A stockholder whose name is registered on the books of the issuing corporation. (See: *Record Date, Ex-Dividend, Ex-Rights*)

STOP-LIMIT ORDER: A stop-limit order to buy becomes a limit order executable at the limit price, or at a better price, if obtainable, when a transaction in the security occurs at or above the stop price after the order is represented in the trading crowd. A stop-limit order to sell becomes a limit order executable at the limit price or at a better price, if obtainable, when a transaction in the security occurs at or below the stop price after the order is represented in the trading crowd.

STOP ORDER: A stop order to buy becomes a market order when a transaction in the security occurs at or above the stop price after the order is represented in the trading crowd. A stop order to sell becomes a market order when a transaction in the security occurs at or below the stop price after the order is represented in the trading crowd. A stop order may be used in an effort to protect a paper profit, or to try to limit a possible loss to a certain amount. Since it becomes a market order only when the stop price is reached, there is no certainty that it will be executed at that price. (See: *Limited Order, Market Order*)

STOPPED STOCK: A service performed—in most cases by the specialist—for an order given him by a commission broker. Let's say XYZ just sold at $50 a share. Broker A comes along with an order to buy 100 shares at the market. The lowest offer is $50.50. Broker A believes he can do better for his client than $50.50, perhaps might get the stock at $50.25. But he doesn't want to take a chance that he'll miss the market— that is, the next sale might be $50.50 and the following one even higher. So he asks the specialist if he will stop 100 at ½ ($50.50). The specialist agrees. The specialist guarantees Broker A he will get 100 shares at 50½ if the stock sells at that price. In the meantime, if the specialist or Broker A succeeds in executing the order at $50.25, the stop is called off. (See: *Specialist*)

STREET: The New York financial community concentrated in the Wall Street area.

STREET NAME: Securities held in the name of a broker instead of his customer's name are said to be carried in a "street name." This occurs when the securities have been bought on margin or when the customer wishes the security to be held by the broker.

SWITCH ORDER—CONTINGENT ORDER: An order for the purchase (sale) of one stock and the sale (purchase) of another stock at a stipulated price difference.

SWITCHING: Selling one security and buying another.

SYNDICATE: A group of investment bankers who together underwrite and distribute a new issue of securities or a large block of an outstanding issue. (See: *Investment Banker*)

TAX-EXEMPT BONDS: The securities of states, cities, and other public authorities specified under federal law, the interest on which is either wholly or partially exempt from federal income taxes.

TECHNICAL POSITION: A term applied to the various internal factors affecting the market; opposed to external forces such as earnings, dividends, political considerations, and general economic conditions. Some internal factors considered in appraising the market's technical position include the size of the short interest, whether the market has had a sustained advance or decline without interruption, a sharp advance or decline on small volume, and the amount of credit in use in the market. (See: *Overbought, Oversold*)

THIN MARKET: A market in which there are comparatively few bids to buy or offers to sell or both. The phrase may apply to a single security or to the entire stock market. In a thin market, price fluctuations between transactions are usually larger than when the market is liquid. A thin market in a particular stock may reflect lack of interest in that issue or a limited supply of or demand for stock in the market. (See: *Bid and Asked, Liquidity, Offer*)

TICKER: The instrument which prints prices and volume of security transactions in cities and towns throughout the U.S. within minutes after each trade on the floor.

TIME ORDER: An order which becomes a market or limited price order at a specified time.

TIPS: Supposedly "inside" information on corporation affairs.

TRADER: One who buys and sells for his own account for short-term profit. (See: *Investor, Speculator*)

TRADING CROWD: The brokers executing buying or selling orders on the floor of an exchange. (See: *Floor*)

TRADING FLOOR: (See: *Floor*)

TRADING POST: One of 18 horseshoe-shaped trading locations on the floor of the New York Stock Exchange at which stocks assigned to that location are bought and sold. About 75 stocks are traded at each post. (See: *Inactive Post*)

TRANSFER: This term may refer to two different operations. For one, the delivery of a stock certificate from the seller's broker to the buyer's broker and legal change of ownership, normally accomplished within a few days. For another, to record the change of ownership on the books of the corporation by the transfer agent. When the purchaser's name is recorded on the books of the company, dividends, notices of meetings, proxies, financial reports, and all pertinent literature sent by the issuer to its securities holders are mailed direct to the new owner. (See: *Delivery, Registrar, Street Name*)

TRANSFER AGENT: A transfer agent keeps a record of the name of each registered shareowner, his or her address, the number of shares owned, and sees that certificates presented to his office for transfer are properly canceled and new certificates issued in the name of the transferee. (See: *Delivery, Registrar, Transfer*)

TRANSFER TAX: A tax imposed by New York and a few other states when a security is sold or transferred from one person to another. The tax is paid by the seller. The current New York State tax is imposed at rates of from 1 to 4 cents a share based on the selling price of the stock. The tax is 1 cent on shares selling for less than $5; 2 cents on shares selling for $5-$9.99; 3 cents on shares selling for $10-$19.99 and 4 cents for shares selling at $20 or more. The tax also applies to warrants and rights. There is no tax on transfers of bonds. The transfer tax formerly imposed by the federal government was repealed on January 1, 1966.

TREASURY STOCK: Stock issued by a company but later re-acquired. It may be held in the company's treasury indefinitely, reissued to the public, or retired. Treasury stock receives no dividends and has no vote while held by the company.

TURNOVER: The volume of business in a security or the entire market. If turnover on the New York Stock Exchange is reported at 5 million shares on a particular day, 5,000,000 shares changed hands. Odd-lot turnover is tabulated separately and ordinarily is not included in reported volume.

TWO-DOLLAR BROKER: Members on the floor of the New York Stock Exchange who execute orders for other brokers having more business at that time than they can handle themselves, or for firms who do not have their exchange member-partner on the floor. The term derives from the time when these independent brokers received $2 per hundred shares for executing such orders. The fee is paid by the broker and today it varies with the price of the stock. (See: *Commission Broker*)

UNDERWRITER: (See: *Investment Banker*)

UNLISTED: A security not listed on a stock exchange. (See: *Over-the-Counter*)

UNLISTED TRADING PRIVILEGES: Stocks fully listed on one exchange may be admitted to unlisted trading privileges on another exchange at the request of that exchange and with the approval of the Securities and Exchange Commission. The approval of the company is not required.

Another type of unlisted trading goes back prior to enactment of the Securities Exchange Act of 1934. At that time stocks could be admitted to trading on some exchanges at the request of a member without application by the company. If these companies today have less than 500 shareholders, they are not subject to the disclosure requirements of the act. (See: *Listed Stock*)

UP TICK: A term used to designate a transaction made at a price higher than the preceding transaction. Also called a "plus-tick." A stock may be sold short only on an up tick, or on a "zero-plus" tick. A "zero-plus" tick is a term used for a transaction at the same price as the preceding trade but higher than the preceding different price.

Conversely, a down tick, or "minus" tick, is a term used to designate a transaction made at a price lower than the preceding trade. A "zero-minus" tick is a transaction made at the same price as the preceding sale but lower than the preceding different price.

A plus sign, or a minus sign, is displayed throughout the day next to the last price of each company's stock traded at each trading post on the floor of the New York Stock Exchange. (See: *Short Sale*)

VOTING RIGHT: The stockholder's right to vote his stock in the affairs of his company. Most common shares have one vote each. Preferred stock usually has the right to vote when preferred dividends are in default for a specified period. The right to vote may be delegated by the stockholder to another person. (See: *Cumulative Voting, Proxy*)

WARRANT: A certificate giving the holder the right to purchase securities at a stipulated price within a specified time limit or perpetually. Sometimes a warrant is offered with securities as an inducement to buy. (See: *Rights*)

WHEN ISSUED: A short form of "when, as, and if issued." The term indicates a conditional transaction in a security authorized for issuance but not as yet actually issued. All "when issued" transactions are on an "if" basis, to be settled if and when the actual security is issued and the Exchange or National Association of Securities Dealers rules the transactions are to be settled.

WIRE HOUSE: A member firm of a stock exchange maintaining a communications network linking either its own branch offices, offices of correspondent firms, or a combination of such offices.

WORKING CONTROL: Theoretically, ownership of 51 percent of a company's voting stock is necessary to exercise control. In practice—and this is particularly true in the case of a large corporation—effective control sometimes can be exerted through ownership, individually or by a group acting in concert, of less than 50 percent.

YIELD: Also known as return. The dividends or interest paid by a company expressed as a percentage of the current price— or, if you own the security, of the price you originally paid. The return on a stock is figured by dividing the total of dividends paid in the preceding 12 months by the current market price—or, if you are the owner, the price you originally paid. A stock with a current market value of $40 a share which has paid $2 in dividends in the preceding 12 months is said to return 5 percent ($2.00 ÷ $40.00). If you paid $20 for the stock five years earlier, the stock would be returning you 10 percent on your original investment. The current return on a bond is figured the same way. A 3 percent $1,000 bond selling at $600 offers a return of 5 percent ($30 ÷ $600). Figuring the yield of a bond to maturity calls for a bond yield table. (See: *Dividend, Interest*)